# BARB SMITH

outskirts
press

Unbreakable
All Rights Reserved.
Copyright © 2022 Barb Smith
v3.0

The opinions expressed in this manuscript are solely the opinions of the author and do not represent the opinions or thoughts of the publisher. The author has represented and warranted full ownership and/or legal right to publish all the materials in this book.

This book may not be reproduced, transmitted, or stored in whole or in part by any means, including graphic, electronic, or mechanical without the express written consent of the publisher except in the case of brief quotations embodied in critical articles and reviews.

Outskirts Press, Inc.
http://www.outskirtspress.com

ISBN: 978-1-4787-9662-6

Cover Photo © 2022 Barb Smith. All rights reserved - used with permission.

Outskirts Press and the "OP" logo are trademarks belonging to Outskirts Press, Inc.

PRINTED IN THE UNITED STATES OF AMERICA

*I dedicate this book to my loving husband, Tim.
Without his love and support, this book
would not have been possible.
Tim, I love you more as each day passes.*

# Table of Contents

1. Introduction ............................................................. 1
2. Opening .................................................................. 4
3. God ........................................................................ 5
4. Rachel's Early Years ................................................ 9
5. Teenage Years ........................................................ 16
6. Brent ...................................................................... 16
7. TJ—Timothy Charles ............................................. 23
8. Mark ...................................................................... 31
9. Mark's Family ........................................................ 39
10. Michael Anthony (Mikey) ..................................... 44
11. April 2019 .............................................................. 54
12. May Rally for Rachel Posts .................................... 55
13. June Rally for Rachel Posts ................................... 61
14. July Rally for Rachel Posts / Barb's Journal Entries ........ 66
15. August Rally for Rachel Posts / Barb's Journal Entries ..... 78
16. September Rally for Rachel Posts / Barb's Journal Entries ... 111
17. October Rally for Rachel Posts / Barb's Journal Entries .... 131
18. November Rally for Rachel Posts / Barb's Journal Entries ... 150
19. December Rally for Rachel Posts ........................... 158
20. January Rally for Rachel Posts .............................. 163
21. Funeral .................................................................. 166
22. Life after Eight Weeks ........................................... 172
23. Life after Nine Months .......................................... 174
24. A Special Note to Parents Who Have Lost a Child ....... 178
25. Family and Friend Memories ................................ 180

CHAPTER 1

# Introduction

SATURDAY APRIL 27, 2019

TODAY IS MY precious daughter Rachel's thirty-second birthday. My five-year-old grandson, Mikey, spent the night and woke up at 7:30 a.m. As soon as his eyes opened, he hit the floor running to my husband's and my bedroom. Thankfully Tim and I were already up and ready for the day, knowing that when our Mikester boy gets up, he's full throttle until he goes to bed at night. He's such a happy kid, always full of energy, and he almost always has a smile on his face. I told him, "Today is a very special day. It's Mommy's birthday and we're going to help her celebrate even though she has to work." We recorded a video on my phone of the three of us singing "Happy Birthday." I sent the video to her with the caption "Happy Birthday, Sweetie," and she replied, "Awww, thank you!"

It started out to be a really fun day. We ate breakfast, and I told Mikey that we were going to head to Mommy's work to give her special hugs and kisses. We couldn't bring any goodies because she had been diagnosed with pancreatitis, and she was on a very strict diet. Rachel was a PCT/clerk at our local hospital in the surgery department. She had a stressful job, but from what her coworkers told me, she was amazing at what she did.

Once we arrived at the hospital, we walked to the family waiting area where Rachel works and asked the clerk if she could tell her we were there.

She came right out and gave us both hugs and kisses as we wished her happy birthday.

Mikey wanted a snack from the vending machines so we got him his favorite treat, M&Ms, and a drink. We sat him at a table, and once he settled down, Rachel told me she needed to talk to me, but she didn't want me to freak out. Immediately my heart sank, but I stayed calm. She told me that after her last ER visit, the labs detected cancer. She didn't have any other information, but she had an appointment with a cancer doctor in a few days. My thinking was she probably had a form of cancer that's treatable and we'll get through this as a family like we always do. I hugged her and told her that I was here to help; all she needed to do was ask. Mikey and I hugged her goodbye and left.

When I got to the car, I immediately called Tim to give him the news, and he gave me his usual reassuring speech about not jumping to conclusions until we have all the facts. I tried to listen to what he was saying, but this was my baby girl we were talking about.

On May 7, 2019, Rachel was diagnosed with stage 4 pancreatic cancer. I have written this book to share her cancer journey in hopes of reaching other families who have gone through or are going through similar journeys. Cancer is a beast, and it's a fight that takes more courage

## INTRODUCTION

than I could have ever mustered up on my own. I am a Christian and I believe in God, who has walked with me through this journey, as well as many other hard journeys that I've been through. He's my rock and my salvation to which I am very grateful.

CHAPTER 2

# Opening

I KNEW WHEN Tim and I started dating that he was the man I was going to marry and spend the rest of my life with. He has such a zest for life. He loves snowmobiling, racing cars, and boating. My daughter, Rachel, was ten when we got together and my son, Brent, was fifteen while Tim's son, TJ, was five. We all blended together wonderfully as a family. We bought a cabin in northern Michigan which allowed us to enjoy many weekends together filled with fun outside activities. Our life was very full, and I'm so grateful for the wonderful memories I have.

Tim and I also share our faith in God. We go to church every Sunday, and for many years we were youth pastors. All three of our children were in youth group and participated in all the activities that go along with that.

In the chapters that follow I talk about our family and Rachel's cancer journey. I wrote this book because I wanted to let the world know what an amazing person Rachel was. I also want everyone who reads this to know that life is very precious and short. If you don't have a personal relationship with God, I ask you to search one out. If it wasn't for the Lord in my life, I would never have made it through the difficulties that life has presented me.

CHAPTER 3

# God

JESUS CHRIST IS the Lord and Savior of my life and I go to Him daily for His wisdom and strength. He walks with me through the good times, as well as the bad. I love the poem "Footprints in the Sand," especially the verse that says He carries us when we cannot walk. I thank Him every day for all that He does for me and my family.

I was raised in a Lutheran church with a membership of well over two hundred people. There were many activities for families to participate in, which was a blessing. I refer to the church as service orientated. They have many outreach ministries in the community that members and families can participate in. This is where I learned to be of service.

My mother took us to church every Sunday, and on our way we would pick up my maternal grandmother, Lucille. After church we would go to the local donut shop to eat donuts and visit with my grandmother. This is a wonderful memory for me, as I was very close to my grandmother.

When I was a teenager, I went out into the world and did some things that I'm not proud of, but thankfully I didn't stay out there long. After my son, Brent, was born, I returned to

God and the church and have been faithfully serving Him ever since. I'm so very grateful to have such a close relationship with God. He truly is my Lord and Savior.

After my grandmother passed away, Sunday mornings were not the same so I decided to look for another church.

I really didn't know what I was looking for, but I set out to explore some local churches to see what they had to offer. I had gone to a Christmas production the previous year that was amazing. At the end of the production, they had everyone fill out information cards and one of the questions was "Would you like to join the production?" My kids were young and I was a stay-at-home mom, so I decided it would be nice to get out of the house and be with some adults for a change. They met once a month on Saturday throughout the year until November when they met weekly to get ready for the production. I had to audition, which made me very nervous. I can hold a tune but a soloist I am not. Thankfully there were four other people auditioning and they let us all sing together. I made the cut and joined the soprano section. I sat next to a woman named Dorothy who was one of the sweetest ladies I've ever met. She was full of energy and loved the Lord. I could see God shine so brightly in her. The director would pray before and after practice to which Dorothy would join in loudly, and I loved it! I was always a quiet person and to see someone praying and worshipping like she did intrigued me.

I talked with my mother-in-law, Patty, about my experience with this charismatic worship. She was raised and still attends what is known as a spirit-filled church. She filled me in on the dynamics of different denominations and told me what I could expect when I visited. I tried a few churches in the area until I settled into a Free Will Baptist church. I really thrived there and so did my children. Brent and especially

Rachel loved it there. I taught Sunday school and performed in many plays. I even produced, directed, and performed in a Christmas play one year that turned out amazing.

Rachel and two other girls, Lindsay and Tracie, would sing special songs during praise and worship. One time I invited Rachel's great-grandma Rice to church, and I made sure the girls sang so she could see how adorable they were. When talking to Lindsay, she said she remembers them signing three songs, "Consider the Lilies," "As Small As I Am," and "Thank You," the one she remembers singing with Rachel the most. She said they also would do sign language to the song as well. I'm so very grateful to have raised my children in the church and that I have so many fond memories.

It was a small church, under one hundred members, and when the 1990 recession hit, many key people who worked for one of the local automotive plants ended up moving to Texas to finish out a few years of employment so they could retire.

Brent was a teenager and he started getting into trouble, so I decided to find a larger church with a strong youth ministry. I landed at a Church of God where Rachel thrived.

The church was large with well over two hundred members. They held services on Sunday morning and Sunday night. Wednesday evening was the youth meeting, as well as a bible study for adults. I made sure we were there for all three services. I was raising my children the same way my mother raised me: if the church doors were open, we were there. I grew spiritually at this church. The pastor was dynamic, and he often brought in renowned guests to speak. Rachel's paternal grandmother, Patty, attended every service with us, which was a blessing, as she is an amazing woman of God. She and Rachel had a very tight bond. Patty married a wonderful man of God, Leonard, who we all adore. When any of us are in need of prayer, he's the first one we go to, as he's an amazing prayer warrior.

When Tim and I started dating I wasn't sure if he would like the church, as he was raised in a Methodist church that was very reserved. The first time he came we were in a revival, which is even more charismatic than a usual service. The evangelist was on fire, running up and down the aisle preaching. I thought for sure Tim would think I was crazy. After the service, as we were walking to the car, he said, "That was great. Can I come back next week?" to which I replied, "Of course you can!"

Rachel especially loved it there. She warmed up to a woman named Ella Mae, a sweet woman who gave hugs freely. She also warmed up to Rachel, and whenever there was an event, I could find Rachel sitting right next to her. Rachel would call her once or twice a week just to talk. I was so glad that she found such an amazing woman of God to look up to. Rachel would invite all of her friends to come to church and to youth group outings. Tim and I would end up driving two vehicles in order to pick up everyone. The youth group kept busy with outings to amusement parks and canoe trips. Tim and I always chaperoned, which was fun. This was truly an amazing time in our family.

I cannot say enough how much my walk with the Lord means to me. I am determined to praise Him in the good times as well as the bad.

If you are reading this book and you do not have a personal relationship with Jesus Christ, I ask you to take a few moments and ask Him into your heart. It will be the best decision you'll ever make.

God bless you.

CHAPTER **4**

# Rachel's Early Days

MY SON, BRENT, was almost five years old when I became pregnant with Rachel. I was so excited to be adding to our family. I had terrible morning sickness, and then without any warning I started spotting really bad and had terrible stomach cramps. I went to the doctor and they prescribed a week of bed rest. The doctor told me it could go either way; I could miscarry or the baby could make it. Rachel was a fighter, she hung in there, and on April 27, 1987, at 6:34 p.m. she came into the world. She was calm and peaceful with not as much as a whimper. She weighed eight pounds, three ounces, and was twenty-one inches long. She had a full head of dark hair, which I immediately attributed to the horrible heartburn I had throughout my pregnancy.

I had two names picked out for her: Christine and Rachel. Once I took a good look at her, I knew she was going to be Rachel. The doctor said she looked like a Raquel as in Raquel Welch due to her beautiful olive skin and black hair. I just smiled. I knew she was going to be an amazing person, maybe not a movie star, but I knew right then and there that she was going to make a mark on the world for the good.

Rachel was a happy baby. I would say she ate good and slept good! She was a night owl; she liked to stay up late and sleep in.

I loved having a girl whom I could dress up in frilly dresses with matching socks, shoes, and barrettes. I didn't care if we were only going to the grocery store; I had her all dolled up every day. Everywhere we went people would stop me to say how beautiful she was.

She loved the attention and would flash them her million-dollar smile.

Once she turned four, she refused to wear a dress unless we were going to church. Thankfully there are a lot of cute clothes for girls that are not dresses. I have to say that this was one of the best times of my life. I loved being a mom; having a son and a daughter made my life complete.

Rachel was a born leader, and she loved the outdoors. Because Brent was five years older, he exposed her to activities before her friends were mastering them.

When she was three, I bought her a bike with training wheels that she rode for a short time. She decided she wanted to be like her big brother and ride without training wheels, so I took them off. She rode that bike like nobody's business. There was a set of triplets the same age as Rachel who lived down the street. They also asked their parents to take their training wheels off, but the next day I saw them riding their bikes with the training wheels back on. I just had to smile, my Rachel once again excelling.

I had an in-home day care that allowed me to be a stay-a-home mom, which I loved. Rachel also loved having kids to play with, so it turned out to be the best of both worlds. I could generate an income as well as be at home with my kids.

When she was 3½, I enrolled her in a dance class at our local elementary school. There were twelve girls in her class, which met every Saturday morning for a few months. At the end of the class sessions, there was a performance to show everyone what they had learned. I was not surprised to see Rachel as the leader in most of the dances.

She would perform and the other girls would trail along behind her. Once again I had to smile and say, "Way to go, Rachel!"

When she turned four, I decided to enroll her in a preschool where she would attend three mornings a week. This was very hard on her; she didn't like leaving me. On the mornings she would go to preschool, she would start crying from the time she got up until the time she was dropped off. Even as an adult, she remembered crying and not wanting to stay. I feel bad that it was so traumatic for her, but I knew if I didn't do it when she was four, when the time came for kindergarten, she would be crying on the bus all the way to school.

Once she got to kindergarten she was a natural. She loved school and loved her friends. Never once did I have a problem with her not wanting to go. She really was the model student her entire school career.

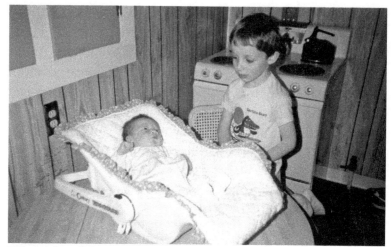

Brent and Rachel

Baptism picture with God parents Uncle Randy and Aunt Trudy

RACHEL'S EARLY DAYS

Rachel 3 months old

Rachel 4 years old

Rachel 5 years old

Rachel having fun riding go carts

Rachel always on the phone

Mom and Rachel at Cedar Point

CHAPTER 5

# Teenage Years

RACHEL WAS YOUR typical active teenager busy with after-school activities, working, and also very active in our church youth group.

When she was fourteen years and nine months, we enrolled her in the Segment One drivers training program. After she passed Segment One, she was able to drive with a parent. Tim was the first one to take her out, but they didn't get very far. Tim said she didn't look carefully before she pulled out of the subdivision and a car almost hit them. Rachel said, "I'm never driving with you again," and Tim said, "Good because I'm never riding with you again."

I realized after their outing that I would be the one to teach her to drive. Oh boy, I thought, I'd better hang onto my hat! We had an agreement from the start that I would not yell at her, and I ended up using hand gestures to tell her which way to go. If I needed her to turn left, I would lift my left hand and point left, and the same with my right hand when I needed her to go right. I took her out driving every day for an entire year. One Saturday morning after she turned sixteen, we met with the driving instructor so she could take her driver's test. She was so nervous that she was shaking like a leaf. All I could do was pray that she passed it. The first command the instructor gave her was to parallel park. Tim had been taking her to the church parking lot down the street from our house to teach her how to park. Tim is an excellent parallel parker.

I don't know for the life of me how I ever passed my driving test because I cannot parallel park. The instructor had some cones set up and told her to park between the cones. She was so nervous that she ran over one of the cones, so he told her to try again. I could see that she was bawling so I stuck my head in the car and got really firm with her. I told her to get it together if she wanted to pass the test. I said, "Rachel, you practiced this one hundred times with Tim. You've got this." Sure enough, the second time was a charm and she passed with flying colors. Rachel was in the driver's seat, the instructor hopped into the passenger seat, and I got in the back seat. I was so proud of her after her initial breakdown; she pulled it together and drove that Escort like a champ.

Once we were back at the school, the instructor turned around to face me in the back seat and said, "Good job, Mom. It's obvious you have spent countless hours teaching her to drive. I am passing her with flying colors; she is going to be an excellent driver." Rachel looked at me and just beamed! This was such a good day for both of us.

I felt like a new person once Rachel could drive. It freed me up to do some things I wanted to do.

Tim gave her the four-door black Escort that he bought for me to drive back and forth to work. She loved that car, especially because it was really good on gas. Thankfully she only needed to ask me for gas money once a week, which I appreciated.

Rachel was not a morning person. She would set her alarm for school, but she would press snooze a half-dozen times. Tim would have to make sure she was up before he left for work. Thankfully I got out of waking her up because I started work at 5:00 a.m.

He said he would open the door, tell her it was time to get up, and quickly shut the door. That way he didn't have to hear her complaining.

My brother Mike's son, Alex, rode to school with her. I asked him once how it went, and he said he learned real quick not to talk to her in the morning. He also said the ride home was fine; she was in a good mood, and they would talk the entire way to his house.

On August 14, 2003, at 4:10 p.m. Michigan experienced a power outage due to a software bug. Rachel was out running around with some friends, and Tim, TJ, and I were headed to a neighboring city for dinner. We heard the sirens and could see that all the traffic lights were out, so we decided we should probably head back home to find out what was going on. I can't remember how we found out about the software bug, but we heard from officials that it could be days before we were to regain power. It was a hot summer night, so we decided we would pack up and head to our cabin in northern Michigan. Tim called our neighbors and they said they had power. We decided to take one of Rachel's friends with us, so I told her they could follow us. Rachel started bawling, and I asked what was wrong. She said she spent the money I gave her for gas at McDonald's and her gas tank was almost completely empty. I was so mad at her. By the time we were ready to get on the expressway, most of the gas stations were either without power or had already run out of gas.

Tim told Rachel to drive in front of us and stop at every

exit to try to find some gas. He told her if she ran out of gas, we would leave her car on the side of the road until we came back home. Thankfully, about twenty miles down the expressway, we were able to find a gas station. It was mayhem and the line out of the gas station seemed a mile long.

People were not being helpful, and Rachel was having a hard time getting to the gas pump. Tim got out of our car and directed traffic until he could get Rachel to a gas pump. There was never a dull moment at our house!

Rachel loved going to church and praising the Lord. As a teenager she gave her life to the Lord, devoting herself to serving Him. In high school she was a peer counselor and also studied nursing. She also got her certification to be a massage therapist, which I thoroughly enjoyed!

I was so very blessed to be her mother and watch her mature into a beautiful woman inside and out. I could not be more proud of the woman she became.

Melanie, Rachel and Stephanie bowling awards

Rachel, Ashley and TJ at Kings Island

# TEENAGE YEARS

Our family

Grandpa Leonard, Rachel and Grandma Patty

Rachel, Holly, Mom and Grandma Mary Lou

Rachel and Tim at the Nascar Race

## CHAPTER 6

# Brent

BRENT ANTHONY WAS born August 5, 1982, at 7:34 p.m. He weighed in at eight pounds, eight ounces, and was 19½ inches long. He was a happy baby and turned into an even happier little boy. He was smart and caught on to things easily. When he was five years old, I gave birth to his sister, Rachel. He was a little put out by all the attention the baby was getting. One morning I took him to the local donut shop, and on the way he said, "Mom, I want it to go back to it just being me and you." I said, "But what about Rachel? Wouldn't you miss her?" He said, "We can always visit!"

Brent was a protective brother when Rachel was in kindergarten. He was in the fifth grade at the same school. A boy in Rachel's class was picking on her at recess and she told Brent about it. The next day Brent confronted the boy. Rachel never had another problem with that boy or any other boy the entire school year!

When Brent was thirteen years old, he started experimenting with drugs. He got busted at school buying a bag of weed from another student. This began a ten-year journey of addiction which sadly resulted in his death at age twenty-three.

His death really tore up our family. Tim and I were motorcycle riders, so we decided to have a memorial motorcycle ride in memory of Brent with the proceeds going to a local drug rehab facility that had tried to help him. We had the ride annually for four years and were able to raise a lot of money. I also wrote a book about Brent's life from my perspective titled *Brent's World*.

The book got a lot of exposure, and Tim and I were able to go into schools, detention facilities, and many churches to share Brent's tragic story of drug abuse with young people. I felt that if just one person listened to what drug addiction can do and decided not to go down that path, then Brent's death wouldn't have been in vain.

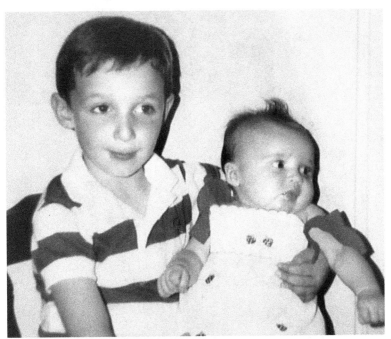
Brent and Rachel

Rachel and Brent at Cedar Point

Rachel and Brent

Holly, Rachel and Brent

## CHAPTER 7

# TJ—Timothy Charles

TJ CAME INTO my life when he was five years old. He was the cutest little guy who loved playing with his toys. He fit right into my busy life with ease. Rachel doted on him hand and foot, which he loved. She would dress him and do his hair for school; she wanted him to look cute. Brent would wrestle with him, which he also loved. They had been known to wrestle everywhere, even in restaurants. One evening we were at the Red Lobster restaurant in our town waiting for an open table, which gave them time to act up. Before I knew it there was a big crash. I looked over to see that they were wrestling and had knocked down a planter that housed a huge tree. It was never a dull moment with those two.

Tragically TJ lost his mom to a horrible car accident when he was two years old, which left his dad to raise him. Tim is an amazing father, and I am so blessed to have him as my husband and a father to all three of our children.

Unfortunately TJ and Mikey would never be able to play together, as TJ passed away when he was twenty years old to suicide. TJ suffered from bipolar disorder and depression, and the grief from losing his mom and his brother was too much for him to bear.

TJ loved the Lord, and he would attend church with Tim and me every Sunday. For years Tim and I were youth pastors. We met with the youth on Wednesday evenings and Sunday mornings. TJ would always help; he loved the kids and they loved him.

When the weather was nice, we would go outside to play games. Usually TJ would team up with the younger kids for fun against the older kids. TJ and his group of kids would always win, and they would shout with glee, hugging TJ as they celebrated their win.

As I look back at all three of my children, TJ was the one whom I feel had the closest relationship with God. I knew that he was suffering, but never in my wildest dreams did I think that he would die by suicide. When Tim came home to tell me the horrible news, I lost it. I started screaming and yelling, pacing all over the bedroom. I kept saying, "How am I going to live my life without two of my children? Who is going to tell me how to live life without two children?" I was completely devastated.

As news spread that TJ was gone, there was an amazing outpouring of love from our small town. TJ knew everyone. The funeral was packed and ended up being standing room only. I was able to meet a lot of his friends whom I had only known from TJ talking about them. One thing that gives me comfort is the fact that some day when I get to Gloryland I will be reunited with my precious son. Oh, what a glorious day that will be.

TJ—TIMOTHY CHARLES

Ashley, Rachel and TJ

Rachel, TJ and mom

Holly Rachel and TJ

TJ and Rachel

CHAPTER 8

# Mark

RACHEL JOINED THE dating website Plenty of Fish in hopes of finding someone she could settle down with. Rachel was an old soul; she wasn't the type to go to bars or hang out at parties. She worked, had a few friends, and loved spending time with her family.

From what I understand, in August 2010 Mark contacted Rachel on the website. I asked him what drew him to her profile, and he said she was beautiful, looked like she was easygoing and fun. They communicated back and forth through email and even talked on the phone a few times. Finally they agreed to meet up at the Outback Steakhouse in Mark's area. He called her two days before their date but didn't call the next day to confirm. He went to the steakhouse and waited and waited and waited some more, but Rachel never showed up. He called to see what was up, and she said, "You didn't call me yesterday to confirm so I didn't think we were meeting." She said it was late and she was already at home and didn't want to get back out, so that was that.

They talked by phone a few more times before Mark asked her out again. He finally asked her if she wanted to meet at

Buffalo Wild Wings restaurant on Friday, August 20th, and she said yes. They arranged to meet at 9:30 p.m. and ended up talking for 2½ hours. He said they talked about everything and that the conversation just flowed. He said he knew right then and there that there was something special about her.

After they left the restaurant, he said he went to kiss her and she gave him a hug and patted him on the back three times. He then asked her if she wanted to go to the Woodward Dream Cruise the next day, but because Mark had to be there by 5:00 a.m. to enter his Mustang in the event, she said no, it was too early for her. She was a night owl and liked to sleep in.

They talked for a few more weeks by phone, but Rachel said she wasn't sure if she wanted to go further with the relationship. A few more weeks went by and something told Mark to call her, so he did and they had a really good conversation. This was a Saturday and he asked her what she did the previous night, and she said she sat around waiting for him to call. Mark said, "Really? You know the phone works both ways" to which she replied, "You're the guy; you're the one that's supposed to call."

Their first official date was that night at a restaurant in a city near Mark called Loco's Tex-Mex Grille. They ended up talking for four hours straight. Mark thought things were looking up, but when he talked to her after the date, she said she didn't know if he was her type. They were both seeing other people at the time, and she thought that maybe they could just be friends.

Rachel ended up going on a date with someone else she met on Plenty of Fish and it didn't go well, so after the date ended, she called Mark and they had been together ever since to which I said to Mark, "Good for you; your persistence paid off!"

# MARK

Every year Tim and I host Thanksgiving for my family. Rachel was there and said that she was dating a wonderful guy. We asked her when we would be able to meet him, and she said she didn't know. When she was a teenager, Tim ran off all the guys she brought home so she was reluctant to introduce us to Mark. Tim asked her if he was a real person and she said, "Of course he is," so Tim said, "Then let me talk to him." She called Mark on her cell and gave it to Tim, which Mark said was awkward to say the least.

Tim and I own several automotive companies, and for many years we would have Christmas parties for our employees. Rachel brought Mark to the party, and it was the first time we got to meet him. Mark says again that it was awkward because Tim was dressed as Santa and handing out gifts to the kids. At one point he made Mark sit on his lap. I'm sure Mark thought, Oh my, what am I getting myself into with this family!

After being together for a year, Rachel brought up the subject of marriage. They both agreed it was time. They went to the Jewelry Factory to look at rings and found one they both liked. Mark bought the ring and it was sent out for sizing; they said it would be a few weeks before it would be ready for pick up. Two weeks later Mark got a call while he was at work that the ring was ready. After work he picked up the ring up but didn't tell Rachel.

In the meantime he called Rachel to tell her that they needed to talk about something. He said something just wasn't right. She asked what it was and he said they could talk about it when they both got home from work. Rachel started to panic and was thinking the worst. Once she got home, Mark had her sit on the couch as he lowered his head and said, "Something just isn't right." Then he pulled out the ring and gave it to her. She called him an idiot and took the ring. Mark said, "Well, is it a yes?" and she yelled, "Yes."

That night we all got together to check out the hall for their wedding reception, and Rachel was as proud as could be showing off her new ring. That was a really good night for all of us.

Every few years Tim and I go to the Specialty Equipment Market Association (SEMA) event, which is held in Las Vegas. Mark and Rachel were going to go with Tim and me, so they decided since they were going to be in Vegas they would get married there.

Rachel and I started planning and had a wonderful time looking for dresses. We went to a bridal studio in our area, and after she tried on a gazillion dresses, we decided on the perfect one. Next Mark got his tux ordered, and where he ordered it also had a store in Vegas so we could return it after the wedding. Rachel was worried about taking her dress on the plane, so she called the airline and talked to a wonderful lady who said that it was first come, first served for storage of big items. They only had one area for extra luggage on the plane and whoever got there first would be able to store their item(s). Everyone else would either have to check it with their other baggage or somehow keep it on their lap. Rachel made sure she and Mark were the first ones checked in so she got the special treatment.

They decided to go to Vegas a few days before the wedding, but due to Tim's and my work schedules we wouldn't be arriving until the day before. Tim booked the hotel for all four of us, but because he was not there when they were trying to check in, they wouldn't let them check in. Vegas is three hours behind Michigan so at one o'clock in the morning the hotel called Tim to see if he would approve their check-in. I was thinking, Oh boy, if this is how this wedding is going to go, we'd better hang on to our hats. It's going to be a windy ride!

When Tim and I arrived in Las Vegas, Mark and Rachel picked us up and we headed to the chapel to pay for the wedding, as well as make sure everything was set for the event. Everything was fine so we headed to dinner and then back to the hotel for the evening.

On the morning of the wedding, Rachel and I went to the hair salon in the hotel to have our hair and makeup done. Then we all ate lunch and waited for the limo to pick us up to take us to the wedding chapel. When we arrived, Tim's aunt Betty, his uncle Ken, and Betty's sister Lil were already there. They live close to Vegas and we were so blessed to have them at the wedding with us.

Betty, Ken, Lil, Mark, and I went into the chapel to wait for the bride. Tim could not have been more proud to walk his precious baby girl down the aisle and give her away to an amazing man.

The wedding was being live-streamed so all of our family could see it back in Michigan. After the wedding was over, Mark's mom called to say that the sun was in the camera and no one could see the wedding. They could hear it but not see it. His mom threw a fit, and the chapel said we could redo it if we wanted to. Rachel asked me what she should do, and I said we are here so we may as well redo it so you can have the video to look back on. So we all piled back into the chapel and they got married again. Rachel later got a kick out of introducing Mark as her second husband!

After the wedding we went to an amazing restaurant for dinner; then the happy couple took off to see the sights.

The next day Tim and Mark went to the SEMA show and Rachel and I had a nice day together seeing the sights and meeting our relatives for lunch.

Mark's brother and sister-in-law, Kate, suggested an Italian restaurant off the strip for dinner and it was amazing. There was a musician who came to every table and sang while playing his guitar. We would definitely go back the next time we were in Vegas.

Rachel and Mark

Mark and Rachel

Mark and Rachel's wedding

Mom, Rachel and Tim

CHAPTER 9

# Mark's Family

DON AND MARY Jane have been married fifty-one years and together they have two sons, Mark and Gary. They are a close-knit family that gets together often. Rachel felt accepted by the family right away and was happy to be joining a family that was so close knit.

I first met Mary Jane when she was in the hospital with a leg infection. She had been battling many health issues for over a year with numerous hospital stays. I found her to be a happy-go-lucky kind of gal, and even though she was so terribly sick, she kept her sense of humor. Gary was also visiting his mom, so I was able to meet him and found him to be very nice. Rachel and Mark were getting serious, so I piped in that I couldn't wait for a grandbaby, and Gary chimed in, "Wait a minute, you guys need to take this slow!" I just smiled. I was sure he was serious about them taking it slow, but I was also serious about wanting a grandbaby!

From what I understand, Mary Jane required a lot of care once she came home from the hospital, and Rachel stepped up to the plate. She would help with dressing changes or any personal care that she needed. One night she fell and Don couldn't get her up by himself, so he called Mark for help and right away they rushed over. One thing about Rachel is she was always there to lend a hand, and I so appreciate all that she did for me over the years. I could not have asked for a better daughter.

Once Rachel and Mark decided to get married, Mary Jane asked if Rachel and I would join her for dinner for some girl talk. We went to a restaurant near where she lived and had a wonderful time getting to know one another. I knew right then and there that we were not going to have the typical, distant in-law relationship; we were going to become friends.

I met Gary's beautiful wife, Kate, at a birthday celebration for Mark's amazing daughter, Emily. Emily got to choose where she wanted her celebration dinner, and she picked a local barbecue restaurant. Not only was I gaining a son-in-law but I was also gaining a granddaughter, and I could not have been happier. We all had a wonderful time that evening getting to know each other and hearing some family stories. They are a big hockey family, they love the Red Wings, and both Mark and Gary played hockey well into their adult life. Gary still plays today, and from what I hear, he's pretty good. Gary also coaches his son Graham's hockey team. Gary and Kate also have a daughter, Hannah, who is a delight to be around.

Mark and I worked for an automotive plant on a shift called C-Crew. The shift consisted of working days on Friday and Saturday and nights on Sunday and Monday. We were both working every Sunday night so Rachel, Tim, and Emily would meet for dinner. They took turns picking the restaurant. Tim was able to really get to know Emily, and he said the times he spent out with the girls are wonderful memories for him.

Emily and Alex now have a family of their own, and we are so very proud of them. Emily is an amazing mommy to her son, Jayson, and I love when we all can get together.

She is a talented artist and I'm always amazed at how beautiful her drawings are when she posts them on her Facebook site. She is not only beautiful but talented. I truly hit the jackpot when I gained her as my granddaughter.

Rachel, Mark and Emily

Emily, Rachel, Mark, Mary Jane and Don

MARK'S FAMILY

Jayson, Alex and Emily

Gary, Kate, Graham and Hannah

CHAPTER 10

# Michael Anthony (Mikey)

FOR MY BIRTHDAY on June 12, 2013, I received the best present I ever could've gotten. Mark and Rachel gave me a birthday card that referenced me being a grandma. At first I didn't notice so Rachel brought it to my attention, and I couldn't believe it! I was so happy. We were all hugging, and I was crying. I couldn't believe I was going to be a grammy!

Rachel had an ultrasound in September to see the sex of the baby, but they only told Tim the results. They made me wait until the reveal party in November, which we had at our house. I bought a bunch of pink and blue baby rattles and bottles, and as the guests arrived, I had them choose pink or blue. We had a lot of pink left over, as I was the only one rooting for a girl. The reason I wanted a girl was so I could dress her in fancy clothes like I did when Rachel was little. Rachel had cupcakes made with blue frosting inside, and we all bit into our cupcakes at the same time. It was an amazing way to introduce our soon-to-be little baby boy.

Rachel was having some issues with the pregnancy so her doctor decided to induce her early. On February 7th, in the wee hours of the morning, I met them at the hospital for the induction. It was a long day with Michael making an appearance at 10:34 p.m. Right before he was born, the doctor walked away to gown up and he shot right out. Thankfully Mark was there to catch him!

After Rachel held him, they laid him in a bassinet to clean him up. When I looked over at him, he had his arms out to the side stretched as far as they would go. It was so cute; it was as if he was saying I'm finally out!

I cried my eyes out as my dream had come true. I was officially a grammy. Tim came in the room shortly after and got to hold him first; then he passed him to me. I love all three of my children very much, but there's something special about a grandbaby. I can't explain the bond that I also had with my maternal grandmother.

They named him Michael in memory of a friend of Mark's who had passed away, and the middle name Anthony was my son Brent's (Rachel's brother) middle name. Naming him after Brent really touched my heart deeply.

I took a month leave of absence from work so I could help Rachel adjust to being a new mom. Mikey (as we call him) was blessed to have such an awesome mommy.

Mikey hit all his milestones and had an amazingly smooth life until soon after he turned four. One morning he woke up with a rash on his body. Rachel took him to the doctor and he was diagnosed with Henoch-Schonlein purpura, called HSP for short. It's a disorder causing inflammation and bleeding in the small blood vessels. It can affect your skin, joints, intestines, and kidneys. The disease caused him to retain water due to his kidneys not functioning properly. He spent most of the summer of 2018 in the hospital with the worst admission being in the first week of June.

On Tuesday, June 5th, I worked my last shift at Ford Motor Company before officially retiring.

My friends Michelle and Cindy brought a cake in for me, which was so thoughtful. I worked the night shift from 5:30 p.m. until 4:30 a.m. and then went home to bed. Around 11:00 a.m. Tim came in the bedroom and woke me up, saying "Get up, get up. Mikey coded. They need us at the hospital right now." It took me a few minutes to understand what he was saying. I jumped up and got dressed, and out the door we went. I called my sister on the way and she met us at the hospital. When we got to his room, it was utter chaos with doctors and nurses everywhere. A social worker met us just outside his room and told us what was going on. Mikey had had a seizure and then coded. Thankfully doctors were doing their rounds and quickly came to work on Mikey. They were able to get his heart beating again and quickly intubated him.

My sister, who's an RN, went into the room, and when she came out, she told me it didn't look good. They said they needed to take him for a CAT scan to see if there was brain activity. Tim and I sat down at the end of the hall and prayed. It seemed like an eternity before they brought him back up to his room and said that, yes, there was still brain activity so they were going to keep him in a medically induced coma and move him to the intensive care unit, where he stayed for three days. Thankfully, on the intensive care floor, there's a Ronald McDonald hotel where we were able to stay. Rachel and I sat with him in four-hour shifts. First she would sit with him and I would try to sleep; then I would relieve her and she would try to sleep. That was the longest three days of my life. We didn't know what condition his brain would be in once they woke him up. Even though he was sedated, he was still having seizures that were being monitored closely.

Three days later they slowly brought him out of sedation and thankfully he was able to recognize all of us. What a relief! He was moved out of the ICU to a step-down unit.

One of the nurses came in to give him some meds, and she gasped and said, "Was he on the bay (what they call the ICU)?" I said, "Yes, he was." She replied, "He's a miracle. We were not sure he would make it." I will never stop giving God the glory for saving Mikey's life.

Rachel was amazing when Mikey finally came home. He was on ten different medications that had to be distributed at various times of the day and night. She had them all lined up on the kitchen counter with sticky notes as to the dosages. It seemed daily the doses would change, so she would update the Post-it Notes. Part of his medical plan to get his kidneys functioning properly was to go through three rounds of chemo. Each round he would have to be hospitalized for monitoring. Rachel took a leave of absence from work, and between the four of us, Mikey always had an adult with him. Rachel and I would take the day shift during the week. Tim would take the day shift on weekends, and Mark and Rachel would trade off on the night shift. It was a very long summer, but by late August he was in remission.

A year later in August 2019 he had spent the night at our house, and around 7:00 a.m. I noticed he was in a seizure. This one was by far the worst he'd ever had. He was taken by ambulance to the hospital where they put him in a medically induced coma for twenty-four hours. When he woke up, he was mad; he wanted the IV and monitors off! They did a biopsy to see what was going on with his kidneys, and it showed his kidneys were only functioning at 50 percent. They put him on twice-daily seizure meds and sent us home after three days. I was worried about him starting kindergarten in a week, but incredibly he bounced back and was able to start school on time. He's been seizure-free since and I'm giving God all the glory!

He still takes one medication for his kidneys and another one for the seizures, but at our last doctor appointment in March 2021, the tests showed his kidney function was at 95 percent. When the doctor told me, I teared up; I couldn't believe what I was hearing. God once again had given us a miracle.

Today Mikey is an active eight-year-old boy who loves Star Wars, dinosaurs, and Legos. He also loves the Lord. We pray before every meal and at bedtime. Every time he prays, he includes blessings for his two beloved dogs, Sammy and Henry. He participated in his first church play on Palm Sunday and I couldn't have been a prouder grammy! God is so very good!

# MICHAEL ANTHONY (MIKEY)

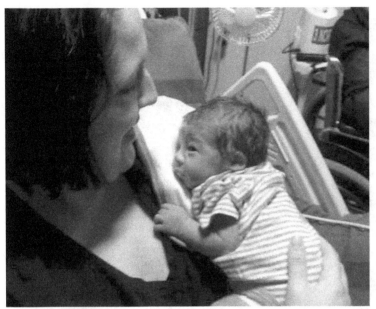

Newborn Mikey

Rachel and Mikey at the race track

Rachel and Mikey at a Christmas store

# MICHAEL ANTHONY (MIKEY)

Mikey and Rachel

Rachel and Mikey

Mark, Rachel and Mikey

Tim, Mom, Rachel, Mark and Mikey at Myrtle Beach

Nic, Nicole and Mikey at their wedding

CHAPTER 11

# April 2019

RACHEL WAS STILL not feeling well and had another trip to the ER. She was in so much pain that Mark took her straight to the hospital and on the way called Tim and me to pick up Mikey. We got to the hospital in record time and brought Mikey to our house for the night.

Once again the ER doctors said it was pancreatitis, but this time Mark and Rachel said no we are not accepting the diagnosis. Rachel said, "I know my body and something is terribly wrong." The doctors did more testing and found two masses in her pancreas.

When I got the call, my heart sank; that was not the result I thought I would hear. I really believed that it was pancreatitis and that with the proper diet she would be fine. I decided not to panic and that surely she would be able to be treated and Rachel would be moving on to the rest of her life...Boy, was I wrong.

CHAPTER **12**

# May Rally for Rachel Posts

SATURDAY, MAY 11, 2019

*Rally for Rachel post by Rachel*
Hi All! Thank you so much for joining this support page that my wonderful sister-in-law, Kate put together! Here we will share any updates that come up. I want to thank all of you again for a huge outpouring of love & support through this difficult time. I'm so ready to fight! I'm ready to receive my port and get this chemo going! #ivegotthis #myboxingglovesareon

TUESDAY, MAY 14, 2019

*Rally for Rachel post by Rachel*
Good news! I get my port placed tomorrow morning & will have my 1st chemo treatment. It's on! You ready to fight with me?

*Another post by Rachel*
Hey there! So I just want to be real for a minute. I am

scared to go through chemo, it's honestly the unknown. Like I've said before, I feel angry, I feel sad, I feel nervous, I'm not having sedation for my port tomorrow so I am counting on pain medication & lidocaine. What if I can't take it? What if I ball my eyes out in front of everyone in the room bc of my nerves? Listen, I know your sorry I have to go through this, I know it sucks.

Believe me! I feel like we are all going through cancer together. Because we are, I need your love, support & encouragement every step of the way and I have no doubt in my mind you'll kick ass as hard as I will. Please, don't be sorry. I've got this! We will have victory in the end because CANCER has nothing on us!

WEDNESDAY, MAY 15, 2019

*Rally for Rachel post by Rachel*

Hey warriors! My port placement went super well today! Only shed a few tears, amazing staff talked me through it and before I knew it, it was over. Only thing I'm feeling is a little pressure in my neck. Made it to the cancer center after, my nerves are easing, my nurse is fantastic and should be my nurse everytime. Still waiting for the chemo to be made up so just getting fluid and anti nausea medication now. So far, so good!

THURSDAY, MAY 16, 2019

*Rally for Rachel post by Rachel*

Good morning! Yesterday during my 1st treatment I had every side effect under the sun! Bilateral eye twitching, nausea, sweating, room spinning, you name it. So I was in there for an extra hour to get everything under control. All the nursing staff was right on my symptoms and did all they could to help. I was, of course super sleepy yesterday. I had a good night last night, took some nausea medication about 3am. It's funny not being hungry in the am like normal. I also have an infusion pump hooked up for 48 hrs.

I'll get that removed tomorrow. My neck feels a little better today, you don't realize how many muscles are in your neck that you use all day until you put your head on a pillow!

Rally for Rachel post by Kate Rosowski

I'm Kate, Rachel's sister-in-law. I may post on behalf of Rachel and her family from time to time. Tonight I'm asking you to please join me in saying a prayer for Rachel. Specifically that she begins to feel better after her first round of chemo. Leave a comment below to let her know you're with her!

SATURDAY, MAY 18, 2019

*Rally for Rachel post by Rachel*

Hi! I just wanted to pop in real quick with an update. Mark took me to the ER Thursday night, I had severe nausea and I felt like I couldn't breathe. I stayed in the hospital for 2 nights and I am finally feeling better today & I'm home resting up. The great team of onocolgist are going to meet Monday am to see what we can do differently for the next tx. Turns out steroids are working for the nausea! Thank you Kate for updating you all the other day and thank you for all the uplifting words and prayers!

TUESDAY, MAY 21, 2019

*Rally for Rachel post by Rachel*

Hi all! My onocologist called me yesterday am and wanted me to get my bloodwork today & meet with him.

I had such severe side effects my 1st dose of chemo. He is now putting me on 3 different nausea meds next round. He wants to continue to stay aggressive with this Tx, we are both on board that we can knock this cancer out! My next chemo is Wed May 28th. Since Sunday I have been able to eat and keeping food down. I'll continue to rest up and keep my mind positive. Today I have lost a total of 36.4 lbs since January. Today Mom helped me clean this house & do laundry. So far, so good!

SATURDAY, MAY 25, 2019

*Rally for Rachel post by Rachel*

A Letter to My Cancer:

It may seem like you have control in my life right now, but you really don't.

Your presence only makes me stronger, braver, kinder, wiser.

I choose how I think, what I speak and how I love.

You will never be able to touch those things. Never.

The fear of your name no longer haunts my soul because I know that my soul belongs to me and to God.

You may take your claim on this frail outer shell but never on my divine spirit that cries out "I am not my body".

My soul will run, leap and tower over your attempts to pull me down into despair.

Those who surround me will fight with me to let it be known that we will not surrender.

Our hearts and souls are tied together in a lasting bond that no amount of your impending growth can break.

You see cancer, you do NOT own me.
I own myself.
And I will survive.
By Ginger Johnson, Founder, HappyChemo.com

MONDAY, MAY 27, 2019

*Rally for Rachel post by Rachel*
Once you choose hope anything is possible
Rachel posted an event she is hosting a landscaping party. She loved working in her yard but is unable to so her friends and family are going to do the work on Sunday June 9th.

WEDNESDAY, MAY 29, 2019

*Rally for Rachel post by Rachel*
Hi all! I had a really bad night last night. My nerves are absolutely going crazy & making my body hurt. I spent 4 hours continuously praying and working hard to keep my nerves and emotions under control so I could sleep. I am so exhausted this am. Mark is going to stay with me today. He is so great at making sure I am taking deep breaths and helps me emotionally.

I have a doctors appt today at 8:30am and we start chemo at 9:30am. I will do my best to update later today.

Another post by Rachel
Still an emotional wreck. Just got ativan & other pre meds. Praying I'll be able to chill out soon. Thanks for all your prayers!

*Friday, May 31, 2019*

*Rally for Rachel post by Rachel*

Hi all! So I had a rough start to my day. My heart rate was elevated 130's while walking. Sitting was 73. I felt so out of breath. So I got a liter of fluid and my chemo pack was removed today too. I am home resting now and going to just relax all weekend. They want me drinking a ton of fluid so my heart rate will be at a safe level. I got excellent care today as always.

CHAPTER **13**

# June Rally for Rachel Posts

Tuesday, June 4, 2019

*Rally for Rachel post by Rachel*
Reminding myself of this all day today. Chemo is not for the weak!
One step at a time. One foot in front of the other. I'm gonna get through this one way or another.

Wednesday, June 5, 2019

*Rally for Rachel post by Rachel*
No matter how many times I break down, there is always a little piece of me that says NO, your not done yet Get BACK UP!

Saturday, June 8, 2019

*Rally for Rachel post by Rachel*
Hello friends! Just want to send out a reminder that our

landscaping party is tomorrow morning! We are so excited to have all of you come & help us with our yard! If you have not RSVP already, please do so, so we know how many hamburger & hotdogs to grab today. See you in the morning!

SUNDAY, JUNE 9, 2019

*Rally for Rachel post by Rachel*
What a great day it was today! Thank you for taking time out of your day to come help us with landscaping! I can't stop looking at this beautiful yard! You all are amazing!

MONDAY, JUNE 10, 2019

*Rally for Rachel post by Rachel*
Dear me, you've been through a lot. I know it's hard but I'm so proud of who you are. You are strong, brave, bright and smart and you were given the gift of a beautiful heart. So keep going strong and try not to stray everything you're praying for is on it's way.

TUESDAY, JUNE 11, 2019

*Rally for Rachel post by Rachel*
Hey all! I had bloodwork & a dr appointment this am. My white blood count is down, but not low enough to not have chemo tomorrow, so we are getting ahead of it and I will have a patch thing on my arm tomorrow that will administer medication after 24 hrs then I can take it off. I will continue to have that for the remainder of my treatments. I have been experiencing right leg pain and swelling in that foot. Dr is concerned it may be a

# JUNE RALLY FOR RACHEL POSTS

blood clot, apparently pancreatic cancer & blood clots are good friends (not today satan) so I will have a doppler tomorrow am before tx. It'll be a busy day, but we will get through it together.

Wednesday, June 12, 2019

*Rally for Rachel post by Rachel with a picture of her port*
I've got a fancy set up today! I'm feeling great this am! Pre meds are running & I'm ready for chemo #3!

Tuesday, June 18, 2019

*Rally for Rachel post by Rachel*
Really having a hard time with this round of chemo. Thanks to my hubby for the update the other day, I couldn't even use my phone. Today I saw my pcp. She reassured me everything I am feeling is normal, she gave me 2 new medications to calm my nerves. Hoping in a few days I'll feel better. I can't even take care of myself without needing help. It's not me! Please pray specifically for my nerves, emotions and to help me sleep. Thank you all!

*Rachel also posted*
She's gonna forever say "I got this" even with tears in her eyes.

Wednesday, June 19, 2019

*Rally for Rachel post by Rachel*
Hey all! This morning I was feeling worse, nausea came back, terrible headache. I got into the infusion clinic today and got a liter of fluid. I am feeling better than I was. Hoping

this is the break I need. Thank you all for your endless love & support. I couldn't walk through this fire without you!

SATURDAY, JUNE 22, 2019

*Rally for Rachel post by Rachel with a picture of wristbands*
Wristbands came in today! $5 each. I have sizes medium & large. All donations will go towards medical expenses. Thank you

SUNDAY, JUNE 23, 2019

*Rally for Rachel post by Kate with a meal train*
Hi all! Kate here. Looking for an easy way to help that has an immediate impact? Would you consider providing a meal for Rachel and her family? Click the link to sign up for a date!

TUESDAY, JUNE 25, 2019

*Rally for Rachel post by Rachel*
Hi all! Yesterday was a very busy day for me & very tiring. I had my usual bloodwork and saw the PA before having my next round of chemo. I am still tachycardic. Running 138 sitting and 158 walking and I am having a hard time catching my breath. Of course! The PA talked with my oncologist and they agreed to get an EKG and hold off on this round of chemo. They will definitely be lowing the dose of chemo for next time & medication that I received for the low WBC was way to high, so next time I will just come in and get ½ dose shot. I am still waiting to hear back from oncology about the EKG.

## *Rally for Rachel post by Mark*

Hey it's Mark with an update: Rachel is being admitted. She has a blood clot in her lungs. They're going to give her blood thinners thru an iv.

FRIDAY, JUNE 28, 2019

## *Rally for Rachel post by Rachel*

Hi all! Boy, it's been a rough go, wanted to pop in and give an update. I had emergency surgery in interventional radiology they were able to get most of the clots our of my lungs, I am on a blood thinner and will be here on out, I also have a filter too so no more clots will travel to my lungs. I was in the ICU for just a day and felt much better immediately after the procedure. I got to the floor last night, I did not sleep well last night bc I am scared to sleep on my left side (my favorite side to sleep on, also when the breathing episode happened) I am also still experiencing shortness of breath which still freaks me out bc of feeling like this for weeks. Drs just came in, I am still in a critical period bc of how hard my body has been hit and my heart is taking a toll as well. This could be because of all that has happened & could be part of chemo. Drs will be talking to my cardiologist today & oncology. Looking at being discharged Sunday possible Monday.

CHAPTER **14**

# July Rally for Rachel Posts / Barb's Journal Entries

MONDAY, JULY 1, 2019

*Rally for Rachel post by Rachel*

Hey All! Just a quick update. I am still in the hospital. Yesterday they wanted to get a stress test of my heart bc it's only working at 35% when it should be working at 50% (both right & left side of the heart) then I find out it's a 2 day test! I mean, seriously?! I just want to go home. So I had the first part this am, it went fine and was super easy.

*Another Rally for Rachel post by Rachel*

Hi all! Boy, it's been a rough go, wanted to pop in and give an update. Cardiologist came in later in the day & said there is no reason to get the second part, so that's great news. Also great news, I am being put on 2 heart medications to help strengthen my heart back up, that will also help me breathe better too. We are headed in the right direction! Huge shout out to Mark who hasn't left my side! There's been a lot of information & more new meds I'm going home on, super overwhelming! Ohhhhh 1 more thing. We are going to flood Heaven with our prayers this weekend! My oncologist wants to do a CT scan to see what's going on with the tumors. The scan will either be Sunday or Monday. We will pray that they have shrunk, and that there is progress!

TUESDAY, JULY 2, 2019

*Rally for Rachel post by Rachel*
We're going home today!

SATURDAY, JULY 6, 2019

*Rally for Rachel post by Rachel*
Hi all. Yesterday was a hard day for me physically & emotionally. I had my CT scan in the am & I was completely caught off guard. I thought I'd be able to walk right in, have the scan & go on about my day since I had another dr appt the same day. Instead I had to drink 2 bottles of the lemon lime drink so that they can better see my pancreas. I had to drink 1 @ 9am and the other at 10am and my scan would be at 11am. I couldn't have a thing to eat after 7am and I sure as hell was not going to wake up before that to eat when I already don't sleep well. Anyways, so I'm laying on the table, 2 nurses tried twice to get IV's, all my veins are shot bc of the pokes so then I had to wait for the IV team to come start the IV. I of course became hot & didn't feel well and I knew for sure I'd never make it to my pcp appt. So Mark went ahead and canceled the appt. I just wanted to go home & go to bed. I'm emotional

about the results, I have all my trust in God that he will get me through this, this is the hardest battle I've ever fought & I am feeling really sad. I have an army behind me, and you guys are the ones that keep me going. Please keep me in your prayers to stay positive & for good results on Tuesday.

TUESDAY, JULY 9, 2019

*Rally for Rachel post by Rachel*
Hi all! Stopping by with an update. I had a cardiology PA appt this am, had a repeat EKG. My heart rate is still high, 120 so we are upping the dose of metoprolol to help with that, that will start tonight. Later in the day I had my oncology appt. We did not get the greatest news but we got good news with it. The tumor on my pancreas & 2 spots on my liver (out of 10 spots) have grown. This chemo regimen is not working, so we are on to the next. I will start the new regimen tomorrow am at 9:30. I will go once a week for 3 weeks then 1 week off. We will do this for 3 months & will have another scan after that. Good news, I do not have to come home with a chemo pack for 48 hrs & I will no longer have the sensitivity to cold! #cancersucks #notgoingdownwithoutafight #wewillbeatthis

WEDNESDAY, JULY 10, 2019

*Rally for Rachel post by Rachel*
Cancer had a good first round. Time for round two. Cancer – your going down this time!

*Rally for Rachel post by Rachel*
Hey all! Today's chemo tx went extremely well. I don't even feel like I received chemo today. My nurse did say tomorrow

& maybe the next day I may experience flu like symptoms like body aches & to look out for a fever. Praying really hard that this is God's way of telling us, yes, this is what you need to beat this! I felt good enough to go out to eat tonight & grab an ice cream

Thank you all again for all you do for us. Keep praying & we'll keep fighting!

THURSDAY, JULY 11, 2019

*Rally for Rachel post by Rachel*
Very tired & nauseated today....

FRIDAY, JULY 12, 2019

*Rally for Rachel post by Rachel from St. Joseph Hospital*
Up most of the night vomiting. Here to get fluids.

SUNDAY, JULY 14, 2019

*Rally for Rachel post by Rachel*
chemo

It's a big tough cure for a big bad disease. It's caring so much about life and those you love that your willing to put yourself through the wringer. It's remembering that, with every passing minute, every day that goes by you're that much closer to being done...with cancer.

THURSDAY, JULY 18, 2019

*Rally for Rachel post by Rachel*
Hey All! Chemo #2 happening today!

I had such bad nausea & vomiting with the last tx. I got an IV medication that will help with that for the next 4 days! Woo-hoo! All pre meds are in & working. Waiting for the chemo to get mixed up so we can kick this cancer's butt! Also, my liver numbers are elevated. I will get bloodwork on Monday. It may be because of the disease, but we need to make sure. Keep praying & I'll keep fighting with you all!

FRIDAY, JULY 19, 2019

*Rachel for Rally post by Rachel*
Hey All! Chemo went great yesterday, only side effects I had were cold symptoms but that is better now. My appetite has not been the best, I take 1 or 2 bites and I'm full or I feel nauseated. This am I had a whole bowl of oatmeal and that went down just fine. I'm so glad! Today, I am feeling pretty good! Thank you all for all your support & prayers. I have the best team behind me! Feeling really blessed!

*Barb's Journal*
Thankfully today was a better day.
Earlier this week God dropped in my spirit the Bible story of King Hezekiah in 2 Kings 20:1–7
He was sick and going to die when God told him that he would give him fifteen more years to live. I thought God was telling me to pray for Rachel to also receive fifteen more years, but He corrected me and said to pray for her total healing. Pray for a miracle. I know that God is still in the miracle-working business.
I started to feel better spiritually yesterday. The despair started to lift. On my way to Rachel's, I started listening to the radio again.

I am loving Sirius radio. I listen to The Message and Kirk Franklin. Yesterday when I was listening, it seemed that every song was speaking to me. I was so encouraged. Then I had a very tough day with Mikey. He's having a really hard time with his mother's illness. Tim and I anointed and prayed over a cloth that I put under Mikey's mattress. We also prayed specifically that God would touch him and help him have a good day. It's 10:10 p.m. and I'm going to try to get some sleep before the Mikester boy gets me up.

Thank you, God, for all you are doing for me and my family.

S ATURDAY, J ULY 20, 2019

*Barb's Journal*
Today was a wonderful day. Tim, Mikey, and I went to breakfast at IHOP, which was fun. We have been doing this almost every Saturday, so the servers have gotten to know us. We especially love Tracy; she has grandkids that she talks to us about. If she isn't too busy, she will sit down at our table and talk. She is one special lady. We are so blessed to have her in our lives.

After I got my hair done, Michelle met me for lunch at an adorable coffee house in my town called Life Is Sweet. I had their spinach and fruit salad, and Michelle had a ham and cheese sandwich with some yummy-looking pretzels and cheese sauce.

After we talked awhile and ate our lunch, we headed to the local flower shop to order flowers for her wedding on August 4th. Tim knows the florist; actually Tim knows everyone in our town, as he grew up here. I'm so excited for her and Mark! I am honored that they asked Tim and me to stand up for them on their special day!

I can't wait; it has really given me something to look forward to.

Monday, July 22, 2019

*Rally for Rachel post by Rachel*
Hi all! I got some really good news today! My cancer makers are significantly lower! This new regimen is working!

*Barb's Journal*
Rachel was admitted into the hospital yesterday afternoon and a day later she is still very sick. She's a short step away from being moved to the ICU. I cried all night and only slept from eleven to three, which has left me exhausted. I don't know how I'm going to be able to keep up at this pace.

Mikey and I visited Rachel, and she didn't look good. Thankfully we got the news that her cancer numbers were going in the right direction. They were 10,000 and have now dropped to 450. I am still in shock. She has been so sick, and when she had the scan that said the tumors had grown, we were devastated. I'm praying that this new chemo regimen works and she can get back to being a mom to Mikey.

I'm praying that I can sleep tonight. It's 10:15 p.m. and I'm headed to bed.

Thank you, God, for the amazing news that we got today about Rachel's cancer marker numbers! Yes, you are still in the miracle-working business!

Tuesday, July 23. 2019

*Rally for Rachel post by Rachel*

Had a rough night, last night. People were in & out all night. Fever came back last night & again today. It got up to 102. Found out my port is infected. Going to have it removed. It will be replaced after the infection goes away. Hemoglobin got low so, I'm getting blood now.

Also have to get a TEE test to check my heart. Please keep up your prayers.

*Barb's Journal*

It's 7:30 a.m. and Mikey woke up with a bad nosebleed. What a way to start the day.

I'm going to take him to an ENT to be evaluated; these horrible bleeds are getting worse.

Thankfully I was able to get seven hours sleep last night, which really helps. I'll be able to complete my daily tasks with ease today.

Not sure what today will bring, but I'm leaving it all in God's hands.

8:03 p.m.

Wow, what a day it's been. Mikey had four nosebleeds, which are traumatic for him. He screams very loud and doesn't lie still until it subsides. I talked to Rachel about taking him to an ENT and she said I could. My sister, Linda, suggested when I take him to the kidney specialist on Thursday, I ask them for a referral since all of his medical treatments and records are with the U of M. It would be easier if I went through them.

Thankfully Rachel is doing better today.

She is still having a lot of complications due to the chemo, but she looked the best I've seen her since Sunday when she was admitted. She also was aggravated, which is a good sign instead of lying in bed lethargic. She was sitting up and feisty!

Her port is infected so it has to be removed, and she's having heart issues so a TEE test is scheduled for tomorrow. While I was with her, she had a blood transfusion. Like I said, she's still really sick, but I was encouraged.

Mikey and I visited Rachel's paternal grandparents, Leonard and Patty, this afternoon. They are very strong Christians and we had a wonderful time talking about the Lord, praying, and fellowshipping.

They prayed that I would have the strength to take care of both Rachel and Mikey. I felt encouraged when I left. God is so good!

### Thursday, July 25, 2019

*Rally for Rachel post by Rachel*
TEE test went good, no infection in my heart. As soon as I go 24 hrs without a fever, they'll replace my port & I'll be able to go home on antibiotics. Probably here till Monday.

*Barb's Journal*
Thankfully I was able to sleep seven hours last night. Woot, woot! My days are way too hectic to go without sleep.

We went to my great-nephew Ian's birthday party and had a great time. Mikey played so well with my niece's three kids. We will definitely be going back soon. She has every toy imaginable, and I enjoyed talking to some adults for a change.

I talked to my dear friend Anna today. It sure helps to have a strong Christian woman on my side, especially when I'm going through a tough time. God places people in my life just when I need them.

Mikey went to the kidney doctor today and got a clean bill of health. Praise the Lord God Almighty!

Mikey went with Pa on his first car tow, and he loved it! When I ask him what he wants to be when he grows up, he says he wants to fix cars like Pa. All three of our children worked in the family business. Tim starts them out young, sweeping the shop and throwing garbage away. After they master one job, he gives them a few more to learn, and before you know it they have learned many skills that they will carry with them into whatever career they choose. Rachel worked in the office answering phones and doing paperwork for years. She also would run customers home when they dropped off their cars for repair. Tim gave each kid their own car to drive and paid for the insurance on one condition: they had to work for it. He also built a custom truck/car with each of them. Brent had a custom Ranger, TJ had a custom S10 truck, and Rachel had a convertible Mustang. The trucks won many awards at car shows. We went as a family to shows in the area, as well as some out of town. If it wasn't in the area, we would stay for the weekend.

My favorite is the car show in St. Ignes, Michigan. The town is close to the famous Mackinac Bridge, and they have the show near the water of Lake Huron. It's gorgeous, and I love all the small shops. While the guys are looking at cars, I will shop till I drop!

TUESDAY, JULY 30, 2019

*Rally for Rachel post by Rachel*
Still in the Hospital. As of midnight, I will have gone 48 hours without a fever. Hoping to get a picc line put in & go home tomorrow. 10 days is enough! Lol! Thanks everyone for the continued thoughts and prayers.

*Barb's Journal*
The day started out as it usually does with Mikey waking

up at 7:00 a.m. We made beds, ate breakfast, and played with toys until 9:00 a.m. when we packed up and headed out the door.

We went to the mall to look for a tan shirt for Tim to wear to Michelle and Mark's wedding. The mall rents car-themed strollers for five dollars, so I got one for Mikey. He was a little big for it, but it served its purpose. I was able to cover the entire mall in no time with him sitting in the stroller. We took a break at the child activity center, where he played nicely with a boy who was autistic. Mikey is so friendly; he never meets a stranger. He doesn't care if you are a girl, a boy, younger than him, or even older; he loves everyone. All of the sudden the boy became very aggressive so we left. It bothered Mikey that the boy pushed and hit him, and of course he had to tell everyone about it. I tried to explain to him that the boy didn't know any different, but all Mikey could see was that he pushed and hit him.

We stopped at Starbucks for a bagel, chips, and pop for lunch. They have the best bagels around. Rachel loves their specialty drinks, so we eat there a lot.

After lunch we went up to the hospital to see Rachel.

She was pretty discouraged as it is day nine of her hospital stay and she wants to go home. If she can stay fever free for twenty-four hours, she'll be able to go.

After that we went to Rachel's house to let the dogs out and let Mikey play with his toys for a while.

Tim called and said he was going to Walmart to get Mikey a pool. Once we got home, Tim said he couldn't find the pool, so after dinner he and Mikey were going to head out to find one. Several Walmarts later they finally found a pool. Tim blew it up and filled it with water. Even though the water was cold, it didn't stop Mikey from having a blast! Tomorrow we are going to the dollar store to get some pool toys. Fun, fun, fun!

WEDNESDAY, JULY 31, 2019

*Rally for Rachel post by Rachel*
Finally home & resting

*Barb's Journal*
The morning started out with a bang; as I was backing out of the driveway, I backed into my sister's truck. I couldn't believe it. I haven't had an accident in years. My car doesn't look too bad, but her truck has a dent as well as a broken taillight. Thankfully my husband is in the body shop business so he will take care of both vehicles, but it sure started my day out on a bad note. Now every time I back up, Mikey says, "Don't hit anything, JaGe."

Rachel was able to come home from the hospital, which was wonderful, but it's hard to see her so sick. She has to have intravenous antibiotics three times a day, so a visiting nurse came to her house to show us how to administer it. It looks complicated, but I'm going to try my best to administer it. Thankfully Tim brought dinner over from a local hoagie shop. Rachel's grandparents Leonard and Patty also came over to help with Mikey. I am so very grateful for the awesome support we have.

CHAPTER **15**

# August Rally for Rachel Posts / Barb's Journal Entries

THURSDAY, AUGUST 1, 2019

*Barb's Journal*
MIKEY SLEPT UNTIL 9:30 this morning. I couldn't believe it. He's usually up and at 'em by 7:00 a.m. or the latest, 7:30 a.m. I was tired so I slept right along with him.

We ate breakfast and headed out to the store. I'm looking for school clothes for Mikey, but the stores still have their summer inventory. I did, however, find three pairs of dress pants for church and some jeans. I also found a really cool Spiderman T-shirt that he loved. Mikey asked to go to the toy section where he found a toy he liked. Before he was born, I said I wasn't going to spoil him but unfortunately I did. We rarely get out of a store without some kind of gadget or toy.

We visited Rachel just in time to administer her medication. I thought it was going to be hard, but that wasn't the case at all. Thankfully she only has to take it for three weeks.

After we left Rachel's we went to one of the Ypsilanti libraries. They have a branch downtown and one closer to where I live. Both branches have large sections devoted to kids. They also have a puzzle for adults to work on, which I enjoy. There are also puzzles at the cancer center, and while we are waiting for Rachel to be called back for chemo, I work on them.

I'm still a beginner so the ones I work on at home are only three hundred pieces. Maybe someday I'll graduate to the thousand piece, but for right now I'm happy with the three hundred.

Tim has a snowmobile race team that he entered into a big race tomorrow, so he'll be gone for the evening. I had a meeting to attend, so I asked a family friend, Audrey, who's sixteen, to babysit for me. She asked if she could bring her friend Bree with her, which I said would be fine. Mikey loves Audrey, and Bree was a fun addition. I'm so very grateful to have someone trustworthy to help me.

I belong to a support group called Proud Parents of Loss. My friends Amber and Josh lost their baby girl, Harper, during labor and started this group for grieving parents. The group meets at our local hospital every first Thursday of the month. They started the group two years ago, and I've been a part of it since its inception. It feels good to laugh, cry, or just sit quietly with other parents going through a similar loss. Even though the circumstances of our children's deaths are different, we all understand the horrendous grief that goes along with losing a child. Amber and Josh are truly two angels that God placed in my life. The path that I'm on is not something I would've ever imagined. Most days I function very well, but when I'm having a bad day, I don't have to suffer alone. I can pick up the phone and reach out to someone who gets what

I'm going through. Having support makes all the difference in the world.

Friday, August 2, 2019

*Barb's Journal*
I didn't sleep well at all last night.

Mikey woke up screaming at 5:00 a.m. with a really bad nosebleed. I feel so bad for him; the bleeds are getting worse. I scheduled an appointment with a pediatric ENT for Wednesday. Hopefully there is something they can do to help him.

We stayed busy all day going to the bank and the chiropractor, and we picked up lunch at the local Coney Island. After we got our lunch, we headed to Rachel's house to check on her. She was outside sitting in the shade. It warmed my heart to see her out of the house. This has been very difficult on her, and I'll be relieved when this ordeal is over and she gets her life back. The visiting nurse came and took her vitals, which were good. She also watched Mark administer her IV antibiotics and said he did a good job.

After we ate our lunch, Mikey and I went to the dollar store to get some prizes for our friends Ethan, who's four, and his three-year-old sister, Brooklyn. Ethan had his adenoids and tonsils out yesterday, so we wanted to send him some toys to cheer him up. They live in Wisconsin, so after we bought the toys (of course Mikey got a few toys too), we went directly to the post office to send them off.

We then headed to Milan Dragway to see Pa race his snowmobile. It was a beautiful night, and we had a great time. Our friend brought his eight-year-old son, William, and he and Mikey had a great time jumping on and off the golf cart, playing tag, and eating ice cream.

Finally, at 9:00 p.m., Mikey and I called it a night and went home.

SATURDAY, AUGUST 3, 2019

*Barb's Journal*

Our day started at 7:00 a.m. We did our usual stuff, and then I dropped Mikey off at his house with Rachel and Mark so I could go get my hair colored and do some school shopping. It felt so good to sit for three hours and get my hair done. I don't think I had sat for that long since last month when I got my hair done.

I went to the Westland Mall and was able to find Mikey a lot of school clothes. It's been years since I've had to do school shopping. The school hasn't sent a list of school supplies that he will need; hopefully they do soon so I can get that out of the way. This will be the first time he has to eat lunch at school, so I bought a lunch box and we've been eating lunch out of it a few days a week to get him used to it. He'll go to school full time from 8:30 a.m. to 3:30 p.m., which is going to take some getting used to. He attended preschool there and really enjoyed it.

After I was done shopping, I picked up Mikey at his great-grandpa Leonard and great-grandma Patty's house. They were outside watching the Willow Run Air Show. He loves airplanes and was excited to see so many of them flying by.

When we got to my house, Mikey played in his pool for a while; then we went to the Dairy Barn for dinner and ice cream. After we ate I let Mikey ride his big wheel around the block. The neighborhood has sidewalks and the roads are flat, so he can ride easily. My neighborhood has no sidewalks and a lot of hills, so we can't ride there.

After a full and productive day, we were headed to bed.

## Sunday, August 4, 2019

*Rally for Rachel post by Rachel*

Good morning all! It's been a few days since the last update. I am home & feeling pretty good, just weak. Mark & Mom have become experts on my picc line...I get antibiotics 3 times a day. We had the visiting nurse out twice this week. Her next visit is tomorrow so she can do bloodwork and dressing change. I've been getting out everyday so that feels good. I've been sleeping well at night. I have an oncology appt Tuesday am to see if I need chemo this week..not sure if they will hold off until this infection is gone. My last day for the infusion is Aug 21st. I think that is all for now. Have a good day!

*Barb's Journal*

Today was Mark and Michelle's wedding and it was magical!

Tim's friend owns a chapel on the outskirts of town. Their website describes it as a quaint little church on ten acres, nestled beside the woods. The owner also owns a floral shop where we bought the flowers for their special day. You can have the ceremony inside or out. Outside the garden is filled with every flower imaginable. They decided to have the ceremony inside, and it was truly one of the most beautiful weddings I have ever attended. The setting was truly magical.

Michelle's son Ken and daughter-in-law Andrea took all the pictures. I can't wait to see how they came out.

They wrote their own vows. Mark referenced Bible stories and Michelle thanked me for matchmaking. For a few hours I thought of nothing but the happy couple, which was a welcome change. After the ceremony we celebrated at a nice restaurant in Ann Arbor.

They reserved a private room for the gathering, and we had a wonderful time talking and sharing memories of when the happy couple first met. One of the gals started clanking the glasses with silverware to get them to kiss, which was fun.

I am so blessed to have been a part of their happy day. God is so very good!

Monday, August 5, 2019

*Barb's Journal*
Today would have been my dear son Brent's thirty-seventh birthday. Last night Tim and I put balloons and flowers at his gravesite.

In the afternoon I went to Rachel's to do some cleaning and laundry. Her visiting nurse came by to change the dressings on her pick line. She said Rachel's pulse and blood pressure were high and she needed to drink more fluids. I made sure all day long that her water bottle was full of ice and water.

Ordered lunch, which was yummy, at the local Coney Island. Mikey and I went for a bike ride around the block and played outside for a while. All in all it turned out to be a sad but productive day.

Tuesday, August 6, 2019

*Barb's Journal*
I headed out early this morning to pick up Rachel for a blood draw and appointment at the cancer center to see her doctor.

Thankfully Mikey spent the night with us, so Tim could watch him while we were seeing the doctor. Tim ended up taking Mikey to work with him for the morning.

This was my first time meeting Dr. D., and I really liked him. Rachel also likes him, and I can see why he's a kind and caring doctor.

Everyone at the cancer center was nice; I can see that they try to make your treatment as comfortable as possible.

After her appointment we picked up Mikey and headed back to her house. Once I got her home, she went straight to bed. I woke her up at 1:00 p.m. for her infusion and then tried to coax her to eat, but she couldn't, which bothered me, but it's par for the course.

Mikey and I went to Wendy's for lunch. While I order the food, he gets our napkins, straws, and lids. I ordered an extra chili for Rachel, but when I brought it home, she said the smell made her sick so I threw it away.

I left once Mark came home from work.

It'll be an early bedtime for me, as I need to pick up Mikey in the morning for his 9:00 a.m. ENT appointment. Hopefully there is something they can do to help him.

Wednesday, August 7, 2019

*Rally for Rachel post by Rachel*

Hey all. It's been a bit since I've updated. Honestly it's hard for me to update when I am not feeling well, so please be patient. If anything crazy pops up, Mark will usually get on and update. Yesterday I had an oncology appt, he says I am well enough to continue with chemo.

So here I am, and they are able to use my picc, so no pokes at all! I am feeling a little nervous today because I never know how I will react to the chemo. Please keep me in your prayers that it goes smooth. #kickincancersbutt

*Barb's Journal*

Mikey saw the ENT this morning, and she suggested cauterizing his nose to try to stop the bleeds. He is scheduled for the procedure on September 26th at 6:30 a.m.

I dropped Rachel off at the Canton Cancer Center for chemo and picked her up three hours later. She went home and slept for a few hours, then unfortunately woke up very sick. The nausea meds didn't work this time.

Tim came over to Rachel's after work and brought burgers that we ate outside. We didn't want the smell of the food to make her any sicker than she already was.

We decided to take Mikey home with us so Rachel could rest. I'm praying she'll feel better in the morning.

Cancer and cancer treatments suck.

THURSDAY, AUGUST 8, 2019

*Barb's Journal*

Rachel had a really rough night, so Mark stayed home from work to care for her. With Mark taking care of Rachel, I decided to stay near my house for the day. I took Mikey for a haircut and then to the park.

When it was lunchtime, I bought a salad from our local bakery called Life Is Sweet. They have the most amazing food and treats. Mikey wanted pizza so we bought a slice from the Pizza Parlor and headed back to the park to eat. We had a wonderful time.

On our way back to my house, Mikey said he wanted to see his mommy, so we headed to Canton. Whenever Mikey asks to see Rachel, I drop whatever I'm doing and take him home. Her illness has been hard on her, but it also has been hard on Mikey.

Rachel looked a little better than she did yesterday but was still feeling dizzy and weak. Mark, Rachel, and Mikey went to Sam's Club for a few hours. Rachel stayed in the car while the guys did the shopping. She said it felt good to get out of the house. I stayed back and took a nap, which felt good. I also sat outside for a while. The weather was gorgeous. It almost felt like a fall day in the midseventies with a nice breeze. Rachel's next-door neighbor Cheryl told me she was praying for Rachel, which I really appreciate.

After shopping they stopped at Little Caesars for pizza and breadsticks for dinner.

After we ate Mikey and I headed to my house where we played outside until Pa got home from work.

I am tired from the busy day but so very thankful I was able to spend some time with my precious daughter today.

Friday, August 9, 2019

*Barb's Journal*

We went to our local bakery for donuts this morning, and then we headed to Rachel's. She was sleeping when we got there, but the noise of us coming in woke her up. I asked her how she was feeling and she said tired because she was sick in the night. She said she wanted to go back to sleep until nine thirty. Sure enough, when her alarm went off at 9:30 a.m., she got up. She has to give herself shots twice daily for blood clots, once in the morning and again at night. After her shot she made her way to the couch in the family room. I filled her water bottle with ice and water and set it by her. She needs to stay hydrated, as it helps with the nausea. Mikey gave her a donut which she was able to keep down.

Mikey and I went outside with the dogs for a while; then we went on a bike ride, which is one of our favorite activities. Mikey rides his big wheel, which brings back good memories of my son Brent riding his. We ride around the block and also to a park nearby.

For lunch Mikey and I went to Wendy's, and on our way home we went through McDonald's drive-through to get Rachel a chocolate shake.

At 1:00 p.m. I gave Rachel her infusion, and at 3:30 p.m. Mikey and I headed to the campground for some much needed weekend fun!

SATURDAY, AUGUST 10, 2019

## *Rachel to Rally post by Rachel*

Today was an amazing day! Thank you all so much for all your donations for the garage sale today.

We are absolutely blown away by the donations. Thank you to Kathleen M. & Kathleen Charlotte D. for hosting. I really enjoyed our time together today. You all are by far the best support system anyone could ask for. Mark & I are truly touched. We love you all!!!

## *Barb's Journal*

Last night we camped in the Irish Hills and had a wonderful time. We ate breakfast at one of our favorite restaurants, Big Boy. Mikey loves bacon and the breakfast bar had unlimited bacon, which worked out for him! I had a caramel pecan roll that was toasted; it was yummy! Tim ordered the breakfast bar. I brought in an activity bag for Mikey that had stickers, coloring books, and markers to keep him occupied.

In the afternoon I went to the salon and Tim took Mikey swimming at the local water park.

Rachel's amazing coworkers had a benefit garage sale for her, hosted by Kathleen Moore and Kathleen Charlotte Dietz, which raised $2,000! Rachel felt up to making an appearance at the sale; she said it was wonderful seeing everyone. She is so blessed to have so many amazing coworkers supporting her.

It's 8:30 p.m. and Mikey is bathed and watching a movie before bed. So very thankful that Rachel is feeling better. God is so very good.

SUNDAY, AUGUST 11, 2019

*Barb's Journal*
Powerful is all I can say about church this morning. Pastor Jeremy preached a message on putting God first. He said, "If you do that, everything else falls into place."

I really needed to hear this, as I have been letting Rachel's illness get in the way of my relationship with God. I easily get distracted by the negativity in my life and forget I'm not alone in this fight. God is right by my side.

When Mikey was sick, two little boys (brothers) from church prayed every night for a year for his healing. This morning they were at church, and Mikey got to meet them. It was very touching. I ended up crying as did their grandma. Mikey went right over and gave them big hugs. I told the boys that when Mikey was at his worst, he took nine pills a day, but because of their prayers, he is down to one pill. God is so very good!

MONDAY, AUGUST 12, 2019

*Barb's Journal*
Today was a busy day. On Mondays I clean Rachel's

ranch-style house. I have Mikey help me; he loves to vacuum. I think it's important for kids to learn how to pick up after themselves and do simple cleaning.

The weather was beautiful so we played outside as much as we could. Mikey has a plastic pool and a motorized F150 truck to play with. I built Ford F150 trucks for a living for many years so, of course, I had to buy one for Mikey.

We went to Wendy's for lunch and on the way home got a Little Caesars pizza for Rachel.

Thankfully Rachel was feeling better today. She was even able to get out of bed and drink plenty of water, which is a huge improvement from the last couple of days.

I am thanking God that we all had a good day, especially my precious Rachel.

TUESDAY, AUGUST 13, 2019

*Barb's Journal*

I arrived at Rachel's house early, as she had an 8:15 a.m. appointment with the infectious disease doctor. We dropped Mikey off at Grandpa Leonard and Grandma Patty's house on the way. I'm so very grateful that they live close by, and they watch Mikey whenever we need them to.

The appointment went very well. Her lungs and heart sounded good, and she can stop the intravenous antibiotics on August 21st. Woot, woot! After the appointment we went to the café at the hospital and celebrated with yummy muffins. It turned out to be a good morning.

Mikey and I played outside the rest of the day, as he loves swimming in his pool and riding his motorized F150 truck. He rides the truck so much that the battery quits and we have to push it into the garage to recharge it.

Today Sammy got out of the yard and headed for the neighbors'. Mikey and I went running behind him. He is such a mischievous dog. Henry's a good dog. He doesn't give us an ounce of trouble, but Sammy I'm blaming for my gray hair!

WEDNESDAY, AUGUST 14, 2019

Rally for Rachel post by Rachel
Hi all! I have been feeling pretty good these past few days. Yesterday I had an appointment with the infectious diseases doctor, I can stop my antibiotics through my picc next Thursday! So that's exciting! Today I got bloodwork & tomorrow is chemo. Praying for minimal side effects like the last round. I hope you all can enjoy this beautiful day today! I sure am!
Another Rally for Rachel post by Rachel
This is tough but so am I

*Barb's Journal*
Today was a good day. Rachel was able to sit outside and watch Mikey play. She also rode with us to pick up lunch. She wanted Little Caesars' five-dollar lunch deal and a frozen drink from McDonald's.
All in all it was a good day, and I'm so very thankful to God that I was able to spend some quality time with my precious daughter.

THURSDAY, AUGUST 15, 2019

Rally for Rachel post by Rachel with a picture of her at the cancer
center
Get packin' cancer, time to move out!

*Barb's Journal*
This morning, as I was reading my devotions, God gave me two scriptures to ponder.

Jeremiah 29:7—"And seek the peace of the city where I have caused you to be carried away captive and pray to the Lord for it; for in its peace you will have peace."

Since Rachel's diagnosis I have been on an emotional roller-coaster ride. When she's doing well, I'm doing well; when she's sick, I'm crushed. Today I focused on leaning on God and His peace, and the day went smoother.

I also read Psalm 112:4—"Unto the upright there arises light in the darkness; He is, and full of compassion, and righteous." I have peace when I rest in God's hands.

I dropped Rachel off at the cancer center for an 8:30 a.m. appointment. Mikey and I went to a local play place called Jungle Java, where he had fun. About an hour later I texted Rachel to see how much longer she would be and she said about another hour. We went back to her house so Mikey could play outside. It wasn't too long before Rachel texted for us to pick her up. We ran through McDonald's drive-through so she could have a frozen drink and some fries. She ate some of the fries but ended up not feeling well and going to bed. I stayed with her until Mark got home from work; then Mikey and I headed to my house for the night.

I texted Rachel around 8:00 p.m. to see how she was feeling and she said better, but I'm not convinced. Sometimes she tells me she's feeling better so I won't worry.

FRIDAY, AUGUST 16, 2019

*Barb's Journal*

This morning, while reading my devotions, God gave me these two scriptures.

Psalm 29:11—"The Lord will give strength to the people; the Lord will bless His people with peace."

Ephesians 5:1–2—"Therefore be imitators of God as dear children. And walk in love, as Christ also has loved us and given Himself for us, an offering and a sacrifice to God for a sweet smelling aroma."

I'm having a difficult time with Rachel being so sick and Mikey struggling, and thankfully God understands and gives me scriptures to lean on throughout the day.

Mikey and I stopped at our local bakery for donuts this morning. Rachel likes the glazed twists, Mikey likes the chocolate glaze, and I like the cream-filled long johns with nuts. Rachel was not feeling well, but she was able to eat her donut and keep it down, which was good.

Mikey and I played outside for a while before heading to McDonald's to eat lunch and play. I was hoping if we were out of the house, Rachel could get a nap. Mikey had fun playing with two brothers. Their mom was taking pictures, and Mikey jumped right in! It was funny and the mom was nice about it. I tried to get him to move so she could get a picture of her boys, but she said it was fine.

I left Rachel's about 4:45 p.m. and headed home for the evening.

Tomorrow will be a fun day, as it's the Woodward Dream Cruise. Every year we enter our Mustang in a designated area called Mustang Alley. In order to get a good spot you have to be there by 5:00 a.m. We meet at Rachel's and head to the cruise with two of their friends, who also have Mustangs. We always have a really good time.

## Saturday, August 17, 2019

*Barb's Journal*

Rachel called at 4:45 a.m. to tell me they weren't going to the cruise because she had been sick all night. Tim and I thought about not going
but decided since we were already up that we would go anyway. With a heavy heart we headed out the door.

We had a good time but missed Rachel, Mark, and Mikey not being with us. Mikey has been to the cruise every year since he was born.

After lunch we left and headed to check on Rachel. When we got there, she was on the couch looking flushed. I took her temperature and it was 98.2. I told her I thought she needed to go to the cancer center for hydration. Usually when she has been sick for a few days, they have her come in. The last two times after chemo she ended up with long hospital stays. With a heavy heart I left Rachel and headed home with Mikey.

We bought Mikey a new bike, and every time he rides it, he gets more comfortable on it.

For dinner we had pizza and pulled pork sandwiches from the food truck at the park. We ate and let Mikey play for a while. He just loves the park.

## Sunday, August 18, 2019

*Barb's Journal*

At 2:00 a.m. Mikey started throwing up, and he threw up every hour until 7:30 a.m. when I tried to talk to him.

He was awake, but something was terribly wrong. I couldn't get him to look at me or talk to me. All he would do is look up at the ceiling, and his eyes were moving around, which scared me. I yelled for Tim to help me, and he came and took one look at Mikey and told me to call 911. Although I didn't have my glasses on, I dialed the number but nothing went through. I guess in our area when you call, you have to put your address in. Tim ran for his phone and was able to get through. I tried to call Mark but my phone was still in 911 mode, so it wouldn't let me. Thankfully Tim was able to call Mark and told him to meet us at Mott's Children's Hospital.

The ambulance got there quickly and did an assessment. One of the three attendants carried Mikey downstairs and outside and placed him on the stretcher. Our friend and neighbor, who is a firefighter, got the call and came right over. Marty was so sweet. He helped me into the ambulance and buckled my seat belt. The ride to the hospital was long, and they asked me a ton of questions. Mikey only came out of the seizure twice—when they placed him on the stretcher, he told them his back hurt; and then while en route to the hospital, they poked him for a glucose read and he yelled out.

Once we got to the hospital they took him to a trauma room right away. They said he was seizing and gave him all kinds of meds. He stayed in the trauma room until they got him stabilized and then moved him to a regular room in the ER. Rachel and Mark came in while he was still in the trauma room. Rachel is so brave. We pulled a chair next to his bed so she could talk to him and hold his hand.

At 3:00 p.m. he was admitted and moved to a room on the twelfth floor. Once he started to come to, he was mad. He wanted to go home, and he wanted all the machines unhooked. They tried to get a spinal tap, but he wouldn't cooperate, so they said they would try again tomorrow.

Rachel and I finally left the hospital after 8:00 p.m. I needed to get her home so she could take her 9:00 p.m. antibiotic infusion. It was hard to
leave Mikey, but we had no choice. Rachel was sick and needed to go home. Tim also went home, leaving Mark to stay the night with our precious Mikey.

With Mark at the hospital with Mikey, I ended up sleeping at Rachel's. I didn't want her to be alone. Besides I needed to keep a close eye on her; she had not been feeling well at all lately.

Monday, August 19, 2019

*Barb's Journal*

I woke Rachel up at 5:00 a.m. to take her meds. Both of us were tired so we went back to bed until 9:00 a.m. when she needed to take another med. Mark called to say Mikey slept well, but he didn't. The chair hurt his back and he had a miserable night.

Rachel had an 11:00 a.m. palliative care appointment which went well. After the appointment we grabbed some lunch and headed to the hospital.

Tim got to the hospital at 7:00 a.m. and helped Mark with everything going on with Mikey.

Rachel and I arrived at 12:30 p.m. The doctors soon came in to do a spinal tap, so Tim and I left. We waited over an hour before Mark texted that we could come back up.

When we got to his room, there was nothing but chaos. Mikey was screaming, and Mark was yelling. They were supposed to put Mikey out for the procedure but decided not to, so they were unable to do it.

All I could do was cry and crawl into bed with Mikey, holding him and trying to console him. Nothing I did worked. He yelled, kicked, and literally screamed for hours.

Rachel and Mark left because Rachel needed to go home and lie down, so Tim and I did the best we could, but it was a complete nightmare. Around 7:00 p.m. Mikey started to calm down and we were able to play a little.

Mark and Rachel came back at 8:30 p.m. Tim, Rachel, and I left at 9:30 p.m. to take Rachel home. She needed to take her meds and get some rest.

What a horrible, horrible day; so glad it's finally over.

Tuesday August 20, 2019

*Barb's Journal*

I woke up Rachel at 6:00 a.m. for her meds. She was tired so she went back to sleep for a while.

I read my Bible in the mornings, and today I read Psalm 16:8—"I have set the Lord always before me; Because He is at my right hand I shall not be moved." I also found comfort in Psalm 16:11 that reads "You will show me the path of life; in Your presence is fullness of joy. At your right hand are pleasures forevermore." What this tells me is that God's got this situation with Mikey and Rachel; I don't have to be moved by the adverse circumstances.

No matter what I have to endure here on earth, one day when I get to Gloryland, all the trials and tribulations will be over. It also tells me that while I'm here on the earth, God will never leave me or forsake me. All I have to do is fully trust that He is with me and will guide me.

Rachel saw her oncologist at 11:30 a.m., which went very well. She's still experiencing nausea and vomiting after chemo, so they're trying some different meds.

We went to Burger King for lunch and also picked up lunch for Mark and Mikey.

Mikey was doing much better, which I am praising God for! We had an uneventful day and were even able to leave the floor. The eighth floor has a gym and tons of games that we played for almost an hour.

At 5:30 p.m. we went to bingo. We didn't win anything. The cute little girl across the table from us won six times! She was so excited! Mikey wanted to yell bingo, but I told him you can't unless you have all your spaces full. It was cute.

Tim came up at 6:30 p.m., which was a big help. They played with the barn and animals we got from the playroom.

At 8:00 p.m. Mark and Rachel came, and soon after that Rachel, Tim, and I left for the night. Mark got night duty with Mikey again.

I'm praying Mikey comes home tomorrow after an MRI scheduled for 12:30 p.m.

Wednesday, August 21, 2019

*Barb's Journal*

At 5:30 a.m. I administered Rachel's last antibiotic infusion. Woot, woot!

Rachel went back to bed and I decided to read my Bible. I read Psalms 42:8, which says, "The Lord will command His lovingkindness in the daytime, And in the night His song shall be with me—A prayer to the God of my life." Then I went to Job 42:10, which reads "And the Lord restored Job's losses when he prayed for his friends. Indeed the Lord gave Job twice as much as he had before." Not sure what God is trying to tell me with these verses. My prayers are for Rachel and Mikey to get well and be able to live a wonderful life together.

This coming weekend I'm scheduled to see the Christian speaker Beth Moore with two dear friends, Michelle and Cindy. I have gone back and forth as to whether I should go or not, but I feel like God's leading me to go. Two years ago we saw her in Toledo and she was amazing. They allow time for prayer with their prayer partners, and I intend to ask for Rachel and Mikey's complete healing.

Rachel got up at 9:00 a.m. for her meds, and then we headed to the hospital. Mikey was cranky. He wanted to eat, which I totally understand, but he had an MRI scheduled for 12:30 p.m., and they didn't want him to eat beforehand. We kept him occupied until 11:45 a.m. when they came and got him. An attendant came in with a wheelchair and said, "I see there are three of you, but only two can come with me." I pretended not to hear her and started walking. As we were walking (Rachel being pushed in the wheelchair by Mark), she said, "If we have an understanding nurse, you can all stay with him."

What she didn't know is that I wasn't leaving.

The nurse in the operating area was wonderful; she said we could all stay. I helped Mikey get into a gown, which he wasn't thrilled about. We had to wait about fifteen minutes before they took him back. We all kissed him and said our goodbyes. We went to the waiting room where Rachel and Mark watched a dog movie and I read newspapers on my phone to pass the time. They said it would take at least an hour, so after an hour went by Mark asked at the desk and they said he had ten more minutes to go with the procedure; then it would be another thirty to forty-five minutes before we could see him. We decided to go to the cafeteria to get some lunch. Rachel picked at some fruit; she isn't eating much these days. She also looked very tired, which concerned me.

We went back to the waiting room and it wasn't long before they called us back. They said only two people could go, so Rachel and Mark went back. About five minutes later Mark called me to say I could come back. Mikey was still sleeping so Mark asked if they could take the second IV out of his hand. When he was out for his procedure, they had to put a second IV in, why I don't know. The nurse agreed to take it out while he was still groggy, so that worked out. About thirty minutes later he was back in his room cranky and wanting to eat. I fed him some ice cream as we waited for his pizza to arrive. Once it arrived he ate the entire personal pan pizza. Rachel and Mark left; Rachel needed to go home and rest. The doctor said Mikey could go home in about three hours, so I stayed with him until they released him. It was so amazing to walk out of that hospital and into my waiting car. I stayed at Rachel's for a few hours and then headed home.

I'm so very grateful to God that Mikey and Rachel are home resting. God truly answered my prayers today.

Thursday, August 22, 2019

*Rally for Rachel post by Rachel with a picture of her at the cancer center*
Half way through today! Only 6 more treatments to go!

*Barb's Journal*
Rachel has chemo this morning so I headed to her house early. Mark took her, and I stayed with Mikey.

She was nervous about her treatment, as she's usually sick for three days after. Before she left I gave her a big hug and kiss, and told her I loved her. It weighs heavy on my heart to see her so sick. When your kids are little and they fall and hurt their knee, you can give them a hug and a kiss, put a Band-Aid on the boo-boo, and all is well. This disease is bigger than I am. There's nothing I can do to make her feel better, and it hurts my heart.

Mikey and I had a fun day playing outside. We went to Wendy's for lunch. While I order the food he gets our napkins, straws, and utensils. The staff is so kind and hardworking. They fill the orders fast, and the fries are always hot and yummy! Mikey loves to dip his fries in ketchup. I love our time together.

Rachel was having trouble with her pic line so she ended up having to stay at the cancer center for five hours, which was a bummer. Once they came home, I left for the evening.

FRIDAY, AUGUST 23, 2019

*Barb's Journal*

I decided to go to the conference after all. Rachel assured me that she and Mikey were feeling better.

We decided to meet at Michelle's house. I arrived at her house first. Michelle and I had a nice conversation; she's my very best female friend. Through everything with Mikey and Rachel she has been right by my side. She's heard me cry, yell, and lose my mind. She's so strong. Not many people can take my emotional pain. One day Mikey and I were at her house and her mom came over. We were all outside so the grandkids could play in the pool when Michelle went in the house for something. I told her mom that I appreciated Michelle and her sticking by me. I told her that she can take my pain, and her mom said that usually after she talks to me and I'm in a lot of pain, she calls her mom and cries. It made me feel bad that I make her cry. She's one of those people that you only meet once in a lifetime. I know that God put us together five years ago when we both were working on the same production line at Ford. Thank you, God, for such an amazing friend. You have blessed me beyond anything I could have ever asked for.

Soon Cindy came and we headed off to Cincinnati, Ohio, to see Beth Moore. Woot, woot!

We stopped at Cracker Barrel for lunch, and it was delicious. I also bought some candy to eat on the way.

It took us over four hours to get to our hotel. We checked in and washed up and headed to the arena for the conference. We got there before the conference started, but it was hard to find a seat. There were over five thousand women there and a few brave men.

Thankfully we finally found three seats together in the middle of a row, but we had to step over about ten people. We all agreed that on Saturday morning we were going to arrive early so we could get some good seats. The praise and worship were amazing, and then Beth came out and spoke for two hours. She talked about Jesus and that he taught from the boat and how the boat was used in a lot of His parables. It was very interesting, and I learned a lot from her teaching.

We left at 9:00 p.m. and were hungry, so we stopped at an Arby's for a snack before we headed back to the hotel.

Once we got to the hotel Cindy noticed that there was a thirteenth floor, and just as she noticed it, a lady got on the elevator and pressed the "thirteen" button. Cindy went on and on about how it was bad luck to have a thirteenth floor. As she was talking, I noticed the lady looking worried listening to Cindy, and wouldn't you know, she got off on the thirteenth floor. I told Cindy she scared that lady to death!

It was a long day so we all headed for bed.

Saturday, August 24, 2019

*Barb's Journal*
    We set are alarms for 6:00 a.m., as we needed to get up early to get to the conference well before the 8:30 a.m. start time.
    At 6:45 a.m. we headed out the door and decided to eat at the Waffle House for breakfast. Michelle had eaten there before, but Cindy and I hadn't. The waffles were amazing. It's too bad there aren't any Waffle Houses in Michigan. I would definitely be eating there on a regular basis.
    We got to the conference at 8:00 a.m. and were able to get a good parking spot on the ground floor of the parking garage. We decided to try to find some seats near the front of the stage. Last night we were on the side so we had to keep our heads turned to see, and it aggravated our necks. Years of working on the production line at Ford has been hard on our bodies. We found a really good spot on the first balcony, in the front row, so we didn't have anyone in front of us, which gave us more leg room. We also sat on the end so if we needed to get out for any reason, we wouldn't have to crawl over anyone.
    Sure enough, at 8:30 a.m. the praise team started, and it was amazing. Beth came out twenty or so minutes later and was still using the scriptures of Jesus in the boat. I loved her message; it was practical and interesting. At the break they said the prayer team would be up front by the stage and if anyone had anything they wanted prayer for to come up. Cindy stayed in her seat and said she would be praying for Rachel and me. She is such an amazing Christian friend. I love her so very much.
    I was directed to a lady who was in her forties with dark hair and compassionate eyes. I told her I needed prayer for

my daughter and that she needed a miracle. I was bawling by this time, and she also started to cry. She said the most beautiful prayer. She asked God to extend Rachel's life so she could take care of her son, who also has medical issues. She prayed for many things for us, but the part that really stuck out to me was for Rachel's life to be extended. After I was headed back to my seat, God dropped in my spirit the story in the New Testament of a woman asking Jesus for prayer for her demon-possessed daughter.

I later looked up the passage and read it in Matthew 15:21–28, which reads "Leaving that place, Jesus withdrew to the region of Tyre and Sidon. A Canaanite woman from that vicinity came to him, crying out, 'Lord, Son of David, have mercy on me! My daughter is demon possessed and suffering terribly.'

"Jesus did not answer a word. So his disciples came to him and urged him, 'Send her away, for she keeps crying out after us.'

"The woman came and knelt before him. 'Lord, help me!' she said.

He replied, 'It is not right to take the children's bread and toss it to the dogs.' 'Yes, it is, Lord,' she said. 'Even the dogs eat the crumbs that fall from their master's table.'

"Then Jesus said to her, 'Woman, you have great faith! Your request is granted.' And her daughter was healed at that moment."

I know that God is no respecter of persons; what He does for one person He can do for another. God healed this woman's daughter, and I am asking Him to heal my daughter. I have the utmost faith that He can do it. I don't know when, where, or how, but I believe He's going to and what an amazing testimony Rachel will have.

I went back to my seat and told everything to Cindy and Michelle. Cindy was familiar with the passages and was with me in agreement for Rachel's healing.

The rest of the conference was amazing. It ended at 12:30 p.m., and we headed home.

All in all it was an amazing two days with my amazing friends. God is so very good!

Sunday, August 25, 2019

*Barb's Journal*

Tim and I went to the 9:00 a.m. prayer service at church, which was amazing, as well as the church service after. God is moving mightily in our church.

We took lunch to Rachel, Mark, and Mikey. Rachel wanted a Reuben sandwich from a restaurant in Ypsilanti. She was able to eat half of it, which was good. She needs to keep her strength up, and it's also important for her to stay hydrated. I make sure she always has plenty to drink. Twice she ended up dehydrated, and it landed her in the hospital.

I took Mikey outside to play and we went for a bike ride. We didn't stay long. I just wanted to lay my eyes on her since I had been gone for a few days. She looked like she didn't feel good, but she said she was feeling okay.

Tim and I got groceries and went to the cemetery where TJ is. I have bird feeders in the tree in front of his grave. TJ loved nature as much as I do, and I know he would love to see all the birds that come and feed.

Tim and I ate dinner at a local steakhouse, which was amazing.

Thanking God for a peaceful day.

## AUGUST RALLY FOR RACHEL POSTS / BARB'S JOURNAL ENTRIES

MONDAY, AUGUST 26, 2019

### *Rally for Rachel post by Rachel*

Hi all! This round of chemo has been good to me, no nausea!

This week I have a break from chemo, I am looking forward to feeling good for a few extra days. This week I have a follow up appointment with Michigan Heart & we are going away for the weekend. Really looking forward to relaxing and no worries.

### *Barb's Journal*

I got up and out of the house at 8:00 a.m. Rachel said she wanted a cinnamon roll from the local bakery, so I stopped there and got us all breakfast.

When I got to her house, Mikey was already up. I let the dogs out, fed Mikey, and gave him his meds.

Rachel got up around 9:30 a.m., so I gave her the cinnamon roll and then cleaned half of her house. I try to get her house cleaned on Mondays; then I don't have to worry about it the rest of the week, as we are busy with Rachel's doctor appointments.

Mikey and I went outside so he could ride in his truck, and I was able to sit down for a minute and read my Bible. After about forty-five minutes, he wanted to go for a bike ride, so we put the dogs in the house and headed to the park. Mikey loves for me to push him on the swings, so that's what I did. After playing we went for a long bike ride.

When we got home, I checked on Rachel and she was resting comfortably, so Mikey and I headed to Wendy's for lunch. Mikey and I got our usual, but Rachel decided she wanted a Caesar side salad. Thankfully she was able to eat it and drink a tall glass of water.

I cleaned the rest of her house, gave Mikey a bath, and then we headed downstairs to watch a movie.

All in all we had a good day, and I'm thanking God for the precious time that I get to spend with Rachel and Mikey.

I headed home around 4:00 p.m. to spend the evening with my amazing husband.

I'm so very thankful for all the blessings in my life; I don't take anything for granted. I know how very special time is with my family.

TUESDAY, AUGUST 27, 2019

*Barb's Journal*

Mark texted me at 6:00 a.m. to say he took the day off from work so I didn't need to come over.

I had an amazing day! I hadn't had a day to myself since April when Rachel was diagnosed.

I ate lunch at our local bakery; they have amazing salads with fresh fruit, and they also have a vegetable salad that's delicious. I then headed to the park for a while. At the pavilion, where I was eating my lunch, there were four middle-school–aged boys playing cards. It was nice to see them outside having a good time.

During my Bible time this morning, God gave me the scripture Romans 8:28, which reads "And we know that all things work together for good to those who love God, to those who are the called according to His purpose." I have to believe that what we're going through with Mikey and Rachel will have some good come out of it. There have been some wonderful people reaching out to us as a support, which touches my heart deeply. The women Rachel works with have gone above and beyond for her. Also, my dear, dear friend Michelle has been wonderful.

She sold fundraising bracelets for Rachel and raised well over $700. At the plant she would use her break and lunchtime to sell them. I can never thank her enough for all she has done.

After lunch I went home and took an hour nap which felt so good!

For dinner Tim and I rode our motorcycle to a local restaurant. It was one of the first times this summer that we'd been out on the bike.

Thanking God for an amazing day and wonderful evening with my hubster. God is so very good!

Wednesday, August 28, 2019

*Barb's Journal*

In my morning devotions I read Joshua 1:9, which says, "Have I not commanded you? Be strong and of good courage, do not be afraid, nor be dismayed, for the Lord your God is with you wherever you go." I'm going to try really hard to be of good courage and not be afraid today. When I think too far ahead, I get fearful. Today I'm going to give the future to God and concentrate on this day only.

When I got to Rachel's, Mikey was already up and dressed. We had a busy day. We dropped Mikey off at Papa and Grandma Patty's house so Rachel could see her cardiologist. The doctor upped her dosage of heart meds. We ate lunch at Culver's, which was nice. Rachel wasn't feeling well so when she went to get her pic line dressing changed, they kept her for hydration.

I took Mikey to his school open house, and we were able to meet his teacher and see his classroom. His teacher is really nice, and Mikey had fun playing with the kitchen and blocks.

A couple I knew from a church I used to attend has had a lot of tragedy in their life. Their son was murdered at a hotel bar as the result of a pool game. I worked with the husband and son at Ford for many years; this happened in 2001. Their other son was diagnosed with stage 3 pancreatic cancer in October 2018. When Rachel posted that she had cancer, his mom Facebook-messaged me and told me what was going on. Sadly, on August 23rd, he lost his cancer battle. This was really hard for Rachel and me. Rachel was the one who told me the news about his passing. We both sat and cried for a long time. What horrible news; my heart is broken for this family.

I went to the funeral home and the parking lot was so full that I had to park three blocks away. They belong to a large church in Ypsilanti, and it looks like the entire church was there. I belong to the church's Facebook page, and they posted that services were canceled so everyone could go to the funeral home to support the family. I hugged the dad and told him I was so sorry. Then I waited in line to talk to the mom. Once I got up to her, we hugged and cried. She told me she was praying for Rachel's miracle, which touched my heart. After I got to my car, I sat and bawled; I even cried all the way home. My heart is completely broken for this family. Cancer sucks!

Thursday, August 29, 2019

*Barb's Journal*

I got to Rachel's house at 8:45 a.m. and Mikey and Rachel were still sleeping. Mikey slept until 9:30 a.m., which is not like him. He's usually up at the crack of dawn.

I took Mikey for a haircut at 10:30 a.m. and then picked up lunch from the Coney Island. We played outside most of the afternoon. Rachel even came out and sat in the sun for a while. It was good to see her feeling a little better.

Mikey and I headed to my house around 4:00 p.m. For dinner we met Pa at the local ice cream shop.

Thankfully it was an uneventful day.

Friday, August 30, 2019

*Barb's Journal*
Tim rented a lake house for Labor Day weekend. Tim, Mikey, and I got there around 4:00 p.m. My sister came out for dinner and then we went for a boat ride, which was nice.

We tried to have a fire, but with wet wood it wasn't in the cards.

Rachel and Mark showed up around 8:00 p.m., and we had a wonderful time talking and enjoying the beautiful, cool summer weather.

So thankful to spend time with my precious family.

Saturday, August 31, 2019

*Barb's Journal*
Thankfully Mikey slept in until 9:30 a.m. I couldn't believe it! Tim cooked a huge breakfast with homemade sausage gravy to serve over warm biscuits. We also had bacon, sausage, and eggs. It was an amazing breakfast. I am so thankful to have such an amazing husband.

We headed out for a boat ride. Rachel was able to go, which was so precious. She's had such a hard summer, it was nice to see her enjoy herself.

Tim and I took Mikey to the park for the afternoon so Rachel could nap. We found a park not far from a pizza place, so we ate pizza and played most of the afternoon.

Tim cooked yummy steaks for dinner. Unfortunately Rachel got sick and had to go to bed. I felt so bad for her. She was looking forward to a fun-filled weekend.

CHAPTER **16**

# September Rally for Rachel Posts / Barb's Journal Entries

SUNDAY, SEPTEMBER 1, 2019

*Rally for Rachel post by Rachel*
Our relaxing weekend was cut short. I ended up getting diarrhea & vomiting last night. I'm at the clinic getting fluids now. Also have a slight fever & elevated heart rate. Hopefully fluids will get it under control & keep me out of the ER.

*Rally for Rachel post by Mark*
At the ER....will update later

*Barb's Journal*
Rachel was sick all night so she decided to go to the cancer center for hydration. After that they suggested she go to the ER, which she did, and they admitted her.

It rained most of the day so Tim and I took Mikey to an activity center called Funday, which was really cool. We ordered a pepperoni pizza and pop for lunch. Mikey was able to play with some really nice kids, and Tim and I were able to sit back and relax for an hour and a half.

The rain subsided and we were able to go on a long boat ride in the evening. We also had a nice fire, but my heart was heavy as Rachel couldn't be with us. Cancer really sucks.

Monday, September 2, 2019

*Barb's Journal*

We went for an early morning boat ride and then Mikey played outside for a few hours. We ate McDonald's for lunch and then decided to pack things up and go to visit Rachel at the hospital.

Thankfully when we got there, she looked the best I've seen her in a while. We didn't stay long so she could get some rest.

We stopped at the store to get the last of Mikey's school supplies. I can't believe he starts kindergarten tomorrow! Time sure does fly by.

Tuesday, September 3, 2019

*Rally for Rachel post by Rachel*

Hey all! Sorry for the late update. Went to the ER Sunday evening, high temp, vomiting, diarrhea, whole 9 yards. They kept me in the hospital because they are worried about sepsis & infections. I received 5 liters of fluid throughout the night & felt like a million bucks. I am still in the hospital because we are trying to figure out the source of infection, still going to the bathroom too much to go home. On the plus side cdiff came back negative. Still receiving IV antibiotics until we figure out this infection. I am supposed to have chemo on Thursday, not sure if that'll be a go or not. I'll update next when I have results. Thank you all for your love & support!

*Barb's Journal*

It's Mikey's first day of kindergarten, and his mommy can't be there because she is in the hospital. I woke him up early so we could get ready and head to Canton. He was not nervous at all, just excited. We had to park in the neighborhood next to the school because the parking lot was full and brimming with cars. It was really exciting to see all the parents and grandparents taking pictures of their students. I was able to take some really cute pictures to send to his mom. It has been years since I have had to get a child to school, but it turned out to be a good day for both of us. It was only a half day, so after I picked him up we went to lunch at his favorite place, Wendy's, and then we headed up to the hospital to see Rachel.

We didn't stay long at the hospital. Mikey was busy and loud, so I didn't want to disturb the other patients. We went home and played outside until Pa came home from work.

It was such a bittersweet day. Mikey hit a huge milestone by starting school, and Rachel was so sick in the hospital. She was dehydrated and had an infection. Life continues to move forward regardless if things are tough or not. So grateful to God that I am retired and that I have an incredibly understanding husband who allows me to step in and take care of Rachel, as well as Mikey.

Wednesday, September 4, 2019

*Rally for Rachel Post by Rachel*
"Hi all Well, looks like I had food poisoning. I am feeling much better. My potassium is low so I am getting IV potassium now, hoping the numbers come up so I can get out of here tomorrow!"

*Barb's Journal*
Today is Mikey's first full day of kindergarten. Woot, woot! I woke him up at 7:15 a.m. He didn't want to eat breakfast; all he wanted to do was go to his house and see his dogs.

When we got to Rachel's, we let the dogs outside and I was able to get Mikey to eat a few bites of a Pop-Tart. Then we headed to school. The teacher has the kids sit outside her classroom until 8:45 a.m. when she comes out and gets them. She has them shake hands or give a fist bump before walking into the room. It is really cute.

I decided to join a gym in Canton so I could work out and lose some weight. I believe it will also help with my stress level. I went to Planet Fitness and got the guided tour from a really nice young man. I used the elliptical for thirty minutes and then headed back to Rachel's. I was hoping she would be able to come home from the hospital, but they wanted to keep her one more day. I hung outside with the dogs until it was time to get Mikey from school.

Mikey said he had a good day, which I was happy about.

At about 5:00 p.m. we headed back to my house for dinner and to see Pa.

Thankfully Mikey was tired from going to school all day, so bedtime was not an issue.

Thursday, September 5, 2019

# SEPTEMBER RALLY FOR RACHEL POSTS / BARB'S JOURNAL ENTRIES

*Rally for Rachel Post by Rachel's*
"Going home today!"

*Barb's Journal*
Rachel is still in the hospital, but we're hoping she'll be able to come home today.

I dropped Mikey off at school at 8:45 a.m., and then I headed to the gym. I'm sure out of shape; just doing thirty minutes on the elliptical is hard. The elliptical I have at home allows me to go any speed I want, but the one at the gym beeps at me if I'm not going fast enough. Needless to say, it beeps a lot!

Rachel called while I was working out to tell me she could go home, so I headed to the hospital.

While we were waiting for her to be discharged, a sweet woman came in to clean her room. She asked if we were sisters, and I said no I was the mom (that made me smile). She talked with us about work and life; then before she left she said she'd be praying for Rachel. That touched my heart. It seems wherever we go God sends angels.

At noon Rachel was discharged and she said she couldn't wait to sleep in her own bed. Once I got her home, she headed straight to bed. When I picked up Mikey from school, he was happy when I told him his mom was home.

Thanking God that Rachel is home.

Sunday, September 8, 2019

*Barb's Journal*
At church this morning Pastor Jeremy asked Tim how Rachel and Mikey were doing, and he said not good.

The pastor devoted the entire prayer service to them. This

touched my heart deeply. After church I took Mikey home so he could spend some time with his parents.

Tim and I spent the afternoon watching a NASCAR race. I also did some reading. The first article I read was about a man from Nebraska named T. Scott Marr. He was found at home unresponsive and was transported to the hospital where his family was told he wasn't going to make it. His family agreed to have him taken off life support, but by morning he was doing better and has made a full recovery. He's now known as the "Miracle Man."

The second article I read was about Kelly Stafford, the wife of Detroit Lions quarterback Matthew Stafford who in April was diagnosed with a brain tumor that required immediate surgery. She went through a horrific medical journey and, as of September, is doing well.

These articles have given me hope for my precious Rachel.

Monday, September 9, 2019

*Rally for Rachel post by Rachel*

Hi all! Just a quick update. Next chemo is next week on Thursday. I still have a little pneumonia in my lungs, I'm coughing a lot more today, praying it'll get better soon. Thanks for your thoughts & prayers!

Tuesday, September 10, 2019

*Barb's Journal*

By far this has been the worst day since Rachel was diagnosed.

After I arrived at Rachel's this morning, I got Mikey up and ready for school. I dropped him off and went back to Rachel's in order to wake her for her 9:00 a.m. shot. She got up but wasn't feeling well at all. I called the cancer center to make an appointment for a dressing and pic line change, which they scheduled for 2:00 p.m.

At noon I picked up lunch. She wanted broccoli and cheese soup from Panera Bread, which sounded good to me. After a few bites, the puking started. It's hard for me to see her this sick. I wish I was the one with cancer, not her.

At the cancer center they gave her IV fluids and changed the pic line dressing. She also met with the physician assistant who was concerned about her rapid heart rate, which she's had since starting chemo. Her cardiologist is watching her closely; hopefully, it won't get any worse. An appointment was scheduled with her cancer doctor, which I'm grateful for, as she hasn't seen him since August 6. A lot has happened since then (a hospital stay, daily vomiting, neuropathy in her feet, and weakness in her hands); she really needs to see him.

At 3:00 p.m. I left the cancer center to pick up Mikey from school. I knew this was going to throw him a curveball. We have picked her up in the past at the cancer center, and it upsets him. He suffers from medical trauma due to his illness. Anytime we go near a doctor's office he melts down. Meltdown is an understatement for what happened after I picked him up from school. Rachel wasn't ready to be picked up, so we stopped by the house to wait for her call.

He didn't understand what we were doing and thought she was already at home, and when she wasn't, he panicked. He went running through the house screaming her name. I told him she was at the doctor's and we would pick her up soon. He was so upset that all I could do was cry. Rachel's critical illness is affecting all of us, and all I can do is pray for God to help us.

During my morning meditation I read these verses in 1 Peter 1:3–6: "Blessed be the God and Father of our Lord Jesus Christ, who according to His abundant mercy has begotten us again to a living hope through the resurrection of Jesus Christ from the dead, to an inheritance incorruptible and undefiled and that does not fade away, reserved in heaven for you, who are kept by the power of God through faith for salvation ready to be revealed in the last time. In this you greatly rejoice, though now for a little while, if need be, you have been grieved by various trials." In the margin of my Bible by these verses I wrote, "Rachel's illness is one of the hardest trials of my life."

WEDNESDAY, SEPTEMBER 11, 2019

*Barb's Journal*

I woke up feeling sad. This is such a hard day for so many people. My heart is broken for them.

When I got to Rachel's, my heart sank as I saw Mark's truck in the driveway and thought the worst. It turns out Rachel had been sick all night and Mark wasn't feeling well either, so he stayed home.

I got Mikey up and off to school and then went back to Rachel's to see what the plan was. Mark said he was okay, just had a stuffy head.

I decided they could manage without me so I headed home. At 2:30 p.m. I headed back to Canton to pick up Mikey from school. Mikey and I did our usual routine and I headed home around 5:00 p.m.

Feeling grateful to God that we made it through another day.

# SEPTEMBER RALLY FOR RACHEL POSTS / BARB'S JOURNAL ENTRIES

Thursday, September 12, 2019

*Barb's Journal*

Mark stayed home from work, as he wasn't feeling well. After I took Mikey to school, Rachel and I hung out and watched TV until her cardiology appointment.

The appointment went very well. The test she had done while in the hospital revealed her heart was working at 50 percent, which is really good. Her doctor thinks her shortness of breath is not due to her heart but other medical issues. He said she doesn't need to come back for six months. Woot, woot. I'm thanking God for the good report.

We ate lunch at a drive-in restaurant called the Chick Inn. I had not eaten there in years. They are known for their shakes so, of course, we had to order two chocolate shakes. I used to take my oldest son, Brent, there when he was little. He loved their peanut butter shakes.

Once I got her home she went straight to bed. I watched TV until it was time to pick up Mikey from school. Thankfully Mikey had a good day at school.

Another day is finished and I'm thanking God for giving me the strength to get through it.

Friday, September 13, 2019

*Barb's Journal*

When I got to Rachel's, I saw that Mark's truck was still in the driveway so I knew he didn't go to work. I went inside and got Mikey up and moving. He was in a really good mood because he knew he was going to Pa's house after school. It's been a long week for him, as it's the first full week of school. I worry about his health with the HSP back. He looks really tired at the end of the day, and he tells me he's super tired. Everything with him is super, super mad or super happy, which I think is cute.

After I dropped Mikey off at school, I headed back to Rachel's to get her up for her 9:00 a.m. shot. She was already up and in the living room, as was Mark. I didn't stay long because I had some errands to run, and then I wanted to head home for a few hours before I had to pick up Mikey from school.

For lunch I went to my favorite store/restaurant in town called Life Is Sweet. They serve amazing salads and all sorts of desserts. They also serve Coke in glass bottles that are extra cold, which I love. I sit at a table closest to the window which allows me to look out and watch the people and cars passing by. I could sit there for hours just watching the hussle and bussle of our quaint little town.

At 3:00 p.m. I headed back to pick up Mikey from school. The weatherman said there were going to be thunderstorms, and boy, they weren't kidding. Once I got to the school, it was a downpour. Thankfully I don't leave home without our raincoats and umbrellas, and by the time Mikey came out, the rain had let up a bit.

Once we got to Rachel's house I grabbed a few of Mikey's things and we headed to my house for the weekend.

Mikey just loves his dogs so, before we could leave, he had to give them multiple hugs and kisses. After a few kisses for Mommy and Daddy, we headed out the door.

The weather cleared up so we were able to sit outside and Mikey got to ride his big wheel and scooter. We have a long paved driveway that goes downhill, and he loves to ride his big wheel up and down it. Once Pa got home, he needed to go to our shop that's located near a Coney Island, so we ordered dinner to go. While Tim did some work, we ate and Mikey played in the playroom. While parents are waiting for us to write an estimate on their car, the kids can play safely in the playroom. Of course Mikey loves to play with the toys, so after he ate I let him play for a while.

As the evening wound down, I was grateful we all had a good day. God is so very good.

SATURDAY, SEPTEMBER 14, 2019

*Rally for Rachel Post from Rachel*
Hi all! Today I finally feel better & food is staying down! This coming week I have an oncology appt Tuesday & Thursday is chemo. Hope your all enjoying this beautiful weekend! Love you all!

*Barb's Journal*
Mikey woke up at 7:00 a.m., which is normal at our house.

When he's at home and doesn't have to go to school, he'll sleep until 9:00 a.m. Tim says he doesn't want to miss anything at our house.

We ate breakfast and played until 10:30 a.m. when we loaded up and headed to Rachel's. She had been home alone since 6:00 a.m. when Mark left for work, and I wanted to make sure she was okay. We took her some lunch from one of our favorite summer restaurants, Bill's Hot Dog Stand. They have been in business for many years. I remember going there as a kid. They serve the best hotdogs and root beer in town. I bought Rachel a coney dog, which she said tasted amazing.

Once we got to Rachel's, I let Mikey in the house and I headed back to the car to get the food. Mikey decided to misbehave and let the dogs out of the house. Sammy ran across the street, running as fast as his legs would take him, to a man walking his dog. Henry stayed in the yard, which I was very thankful for. I ran into the house and put the food on the table and headed for the door to see if I could catch the dogs. Henry is such a good dog; he came right back into the house. Sammy was a different story. He was having too much fun with the other dog across the street. I yelled and yelled, and he finally came back home and I was able to get him into the house. I was not very happy with Mikey; he knows better than to let the dogs get out. Life with a five-year-old can be challenging.

We ate lunch and then Mikey, the dogs, and I headed to the backyard for some outside fun. Just as I sat down, Mikey came around the corner to tell me the dogs broke through the fence and into the neighbors' backyard. I couldn't believe it. I tried to get them to come back through the hole in the fence, but those stinkers would not do it. I yelled and yelled but they acted like they didn't hear me, so I went inside the house, got the leash, and went to the neighbors' house.

Once I got there, I told them, "Please don't be mad at me. I'm just the grandma." I told them about Rachel being sick and that I was trying to fill in as best as I could. They were wonderful and led me to their backyard so I could get the dogs. The dogs are too strong for me to take together so I had to take them home one at a time. I was so very thankful to God that they were so kind to me.

I had a hair appointment scheduled for late afternoon, so after I was sure that Rachel was okay, I headed to my appointment.

After I got my hair done, I headed to one of my favorite parks. It has amazing walking paths that I so enjoy. The weather was perfect in the midseventies with a nice breeze. After my walk I started to head back to my car when I met a lovely lady who was weeding the flower beds. I told her she was doing an amazing job, and I sat down so we could chat. She was so kind and loving. She told me her name was Naida and she was seventy-six years old, which surprised me because she didn't look a day over sixty. She asked how my day was going, and I burst into tears. I told her about Rachel, and she immediately gave me a hug and told me she was so sorry. She said she goes to the Marble Methodist Church and their service is at 10:00 a.m. Sunday and she would love to see me sometime. I have to say that God is showing up and showing out in a big way for me lately. I know He placed Naida in my path because He knew I needed a hug and to show me that people really do care about me.

SUNDAY, SEPTEMBER 15, 2019

*Barb's Journal*
Church was amazing this morning; we celebrated seven years. Tim and I have been attending for five years.

When we started attending, we were meeting at the Rave movie theater. Two years ago we bought a building in Ann Arbor, where we are located now. The worship was amazing and the sermon spot on. I really needed to hear what Pastor Jeremy had to say. Mikey also was good in his class, which helped. One of his teachers, Jared, is amazing, and when I dropped Mikey off, he asked me how I was and I said "terrible." He said of course you're feeling terrible; you're going through a really terrible time. He gave me a big hug and talked to me for a while. I so appreciated his kindness. Like I said yesterday, God is placing kind and loving people in my path, and I'm so grateful.

## Monday, September 16, 2019

*Rally for Rachel post by Rachel*
"I am too positive to be doubtful, too optimistic to be fearful, and too determined to be defeated"

*Barb's Journal*
Mikey was in a good mood when I woke him up. He was excited to get his day started. After I dropped him off at school, I went back to Rachel's. She was up and had already administered her shot. She said she was feeling pretty good. She wanted some fruit for breakfast, and she was able to keep it down. She even felt good enough to sit up and watch some TV. We had a nice morning together talking about Mikey and watching talk shows. Rachel said chicken salad sounded good for lunch so that is what we had.

After lunch she took a nap in bed and I watched TV until it was time to get Mikey from school. Mikey had a good day at school, which was awesome.

Thank you, God, for an amazing day. It warms my heart when my daughter and grandson are doing well.

## Tuesday, September 17, 2019

*Barb's Journal*
I got to Rachel's at my usual 7:30 a.m. and Mikey was awake and ready to start his day. I love taking him to school in the morning. He sits down outside his classroom until the bell rings. At 8:45 a.m. his teacher comes out and has the students stand up and, one by one, they head into the classroom. She has them give her a fist bump, a hug, or a high five. Mikey always gives her a fist bump. As he's walking in, I throw him kisses, which makes him smile.

I headed back to Rachel's, and when I got there, she was already up and said she'd been up most of the night with pancreatic pain. She didn't want any breakfast and ended up going back to bed. I'm devastated. This isn't good at all. She hasn't had this kind of pain in over a month.

I took Rachel to her lab appointment at twelve fifteen and then to an appointment with her oncologist, Dr. D, who's amazing. He gave us her treatment plan, which consists of chemo for three weeks; then she'll have scans to see if the tumors in her pancreas have shrunk.

We ate lunch in between appointments and were able to have some really good conversation. I have really enjoyed spending quality time with her.

With Mikey in school all day I can take her to all her appointments, which also allows me to hear what the doctors say firsthand.

WEDNESDAY, SEPTEMBER 18, 2019

*Rally for Rachel post by Rachel*

Hi all! I had my onocology appt yesterday. We have a plan of doing the next cycle (chemo once a week for 3 weeks then a week off) on October 2 I'll have a CT scan for staging. Then I'll have a follow up with the doctor & discuss where to go from there.

I just received a call from the office. My cancer numbers were about 9500 in august & now it's around 4500! God is so good, isn't he"! I haven't even had chemo in 3 weeks!

*Barb's Journal*

Mikey was in a good mood when I woke him up. He's been going to bed earlier so it's been easier to get him up and going.

At 9:30 a.m. Rachel got a call from the oncology office with her cancer numbers. Zero means you have no cancer in your body. In August her number was 9,500; her test from yesterday says her number is 4,500. I couldn't believe what I was hearing. Once I took it in, I started crying and couldn't stop. I knew I needed to call Tim, so I went outside to compose myself. Tim said, "Praise the Lord." I also called my bestie, Michelle, and she was excited and said, "God is answering prayers." Since we got the phone call I have been on cloud nine. God is amazing, and I am giving Him all the praise and glory for the amazing report! Thank you, God, for hearing our prayers!

Thursday, September 19, 2019

Rally for Rachel post by Rachel
Look who I have with me at chemo today! (It's a picture of her and I)
We both are tired today. Had a hard time sleeping last night, I always get worked up about having chemo because I never know how it's going to treat me. Just received all my pre meds and chemo will follow. Have a great day!

*Barb's Journal*
I arrived at Rachel's at my usual 7:30 a.m. and got Mikey up and off to school. I headed back to Rachel's to get her for her 9:30 a.m. chemo appointment. Chemo day is always hard on her; it causes her to not sleep well the night before. I also didn't get a good night's rest, as I had her on my mind all night. She was feeling sick to her stomach and didn't want to eat breakfast, but I got her to drink a protein shake and then we headed to the cancer center.
This is the first time I was able to stay with her for her entire treatment. Now that Mikey's in school all day, it has freed

me up to be with her. Everyone is so kind, and Rachel's nurse Deana is amazing. She is kind, funny, and an amazing nurse. I can see why Rachel speaks so highly of her.

Friday, September 20, 2019

*Rally for Rachel post by Rachel*
Chemo knocked me down yesterday & today I'm back up. I am able to eat & keeping everything down so far. All these prayers are working! Let's keep flooding Heaven with all our prayers.

Tuesday, September 24, 2019

*Rally for Rachel post by Rachel*
Hi all! Well, so far so good with the chemo! I only had 1 bad day and that was the day I got chemo, I had a full body ache, so I took pain meds and went to bed & that worked. Tomorrow morning I will have chemo again. This weekend will be pretty special, Michael will be in his first wedding as a ring bearer. We are so excited, and honored to be apart of this special day. Praying this chemo tomorrow will treat me just as well so I'm able to go. Have a great day friends!

Thursday, September 26, 2019

*Rally for Rachel post by Rachel*
Hi all! Chemo itself went well yesterday & got our of there with no issues! (Picc worked like it was suppose to, heart rate was good & bloodwork was great) until I was home for a bit, full body ache & I couldn't get comfortable.

Thankfully that only lasted a bit. This morning I am feeling good, just fighting a little heartburn. Have a great day!

Friday, September 27, 2019

*Barb's Journal*
When I got to Rachel's, Mikey was already up and in a really good mood, which is good because this weekend is our dear friends Nic and Nicole's wedding. Tim is a groomsman and Mikey is the ring bearer. I bought Mikey the cutest blue suit with suspenders, a bow tie, and argyle socks to match. I also bought him some goodie bags that I filled with stickers, markers, and Hot Wheels to keep him busy tonight at the rehearsal, as well as tomorrow after the wedding.

Rachel is doing really well today. She ate breakfast and lunch without incident. She's planning to go with Mikey and me to the rehearsal dinner, and I'm so excited. Her mother-in-law, Mary Jane, loaned her a wheelchair, which is light, so I put it in the trunk of my car to use at the dinner.

The dinner was amazing. It was in a barn on a horse farm. Mikey loved the horses and wanted to ride them. I told him if he was good, I would take him to pet the horses tomorrow after the wedding. I always have to have something up my sleeve to get him to behave. It rained the entire time we were there, so Mikey didn't get a chance to rehearse. Hopefully he'll be able to tomorrow before the wedding. Everyone was so happy to see Rachel and spend some time with her. She's been sick all summer so she hasn't been to any social events.

Thanking God for an amazing day.

Saturday, September 28, 2019

## Barb's Journal

Rachel woke up sick this morning and was unable to attend Nic and Nicole's wedding. We were all very disappointed. I picked up Mikey and met Tim at the wedding venue. Tim was already there rehearsing. Mikey was his usual Mikey self. When it came time for him to give the pillow and rings to Tim, wouldn't you know, he threw the pillow instead of nicely handing it to Tim.

Everyone laughed while I was mortified. He probably won't be asked to participate in another wedding anytime soon! After the ceremony I took Mikey home and then went back for the reception. The reception was outside in a huge tent. After we ate dinner, everyone moved to the barn for dancing. We all had a wonderful time. It was by far the most beautiful wedding and reception I've ever attended. I wish the newlyweds nothing but blessings and happiness for years to come.

MONDAY, SEPTEMBER 30, 2019

## Rally for Rachel post by Rachel

Hi all! I have a busy week this week. Today I have a palliative care appt, hoping to get Rx for heartburn & belly issues. Tomorrow I will have my picc care. Wednesday is the big day, my CT to see where we're at with the tumors. Praying so hard they have shrunk and I won't need many more chemo Tx's. Thursday is chemo. Whew! I will of course be resting in between. I hope you all have a great day!

## Another Rally for Rachel post by Rachel's

Picture of Rachel with a shaved head.

Well, I did it! Thank you Jackie for shaving what was left of my hair. It's a relief to have it gone & not in my way. This was a very hard decision to make but I'm glad it's done.

129

*Barb's Journal*

Rachel had an appointment with the palliative care doctor today, and it was hard for me to hear what she had to say. She asked Rachel if she had thought about assigning a person to handle decisions if she was unable to make them.

Mark, Rachel, and I talked about the advanced directive, and we decided Mark and I will make the decisions for her together. We need to have two nonfamily witnesses, so we asked Rachel's amazing neighbors Sheryl and Ed to be our witnesses. It hurt my heart to be talking about this, but I also know that I want her wishes honored. She told me she wants everything possible done to save her, and in the event they can't, she wants to donate all her organs. This makes me cry. I just want my precious daughter happy and healthy. I don't want to be talking about donating anything.

Rachel also told the doctor that she's having pancreas and liver pain. This is the first time I'm hearing about her pain, and it scares me.

Tomorrow she's scheduled for a scan to see if her pancreas and liver tumors are responding to chemo. I'm praying we get a good report and that we know the results by Friday, as I would hate to have to worry about it all weekend.

My heart is heavy right now; hoping I'll be able to get some sleep tonight as I'm physically, emotionally, and mentally exhausted.

CHAPTER **17**

# October Rally for Rachel Posts / Barb's Journal Entries

TUESDAY, OCTOBER 1, 2019

*Barb's Journal*
I GOT MIKEY off to school and headed back to Rachel's to wake her up for her 9:00 a.m. shot. She was feeling good so I decided to head to the gym. Working out three to four days a week has really helped my anxiety level.

When I got back to the house, Rachel was still doing good and even felt like having a cheesesteak hoagie from our local hoagie shop. Within forty minutes Door Dash delivered our lunch and it was delicious.

At 2:30 p.m. we headed to the cancer center to get her pic line flushed and some blood work done. I told her to wait a few minutes before coming out to my car, as I wanted to clear out everything I had sitting in the passenger seat. I turned around to see if she was coming, and I panicked as I saw her sitting on the ground crying. She had no feeling in her toes and couldn't gauge the steps and fell. I looked across the street as her amazing neighbor Jaclyn was leaving her house, so I yelled to her and asked if her husband, Ken, was home and, if so, could they help me. Thankfully Ken was home so they both came right over. He was able to help Rachel off the ground and into the wheelchair. I got her some paper towels to help stop the bleeding in her hand, but because she's on blood thinners I couldn't get the bleeding to stop.

Rachel called the oncology office and they told her as long as she didn't hit her head she'd be fine. I got her into my car and took her to the cancer center for her appointment. I also knew that they would help with her bleeding hand.

She ended up going to Urgent Care and they X-rayed her ankle, which thankfully isn't broke. They also were able to get her hand to stop bleeding, which was a big concern for me.

I'm thanking God that her ankle's not broken, and though she's shaken up, she's okay. It's never a dull moment around here!

Wednesday, October 2, 2019

*Rally for Rachel post by Rachel*
Hi all! My neuropathy in my feet are getting worse & I took a fall yesterday because of it. I sprained my left ankle & skinned up my left palm on the way down. Thankfully I was not alone & my neighbors came over to help me up. Such a struggle when your weak. I feel like when I take 2 steps forward I take 3 steps back. This beast is really getting to me. I just want a break. Mark bought me a cane yesterday and that is helping with getting around. #thestruggleisreal

*Rally for Rachel post by Rachel*
This is perfect for me today.

You know great things are coming when everything seems to be going wrong. Old energy is clearing out for new energy to enter. Be patient!

*Barb's Journal*
Today Rachel is scheduled for a scan to see if the chemo is shrinking the tumors in her pancreas and liver. I have a lot of anxiety for her as the scan is very hard on her physically. She has to drink contrast, which gives her severe nausea from the taste and smell. I'm also anxious to see where she stands with the tumors. She told the doctor that she was having pain in her pancreas and liver area, which scares me. There's a lot riding on the results of this scan.

On the positive side, we're so grateful to have a wonderful support system. Rachel has many friends who are praying for her and I do as well. My bestie, Michelle, is my rock. I can call her with any of my concerns, which is what I did this morning on my way to Rachel's and I ended up crying my eyes out. I thank God for such an amazing friend.

THURSDAY, OCTOBER 3, 2019

*Rally for Rachel by Rachel*
Hi all! At chemo this morning. The doctor has decided to not proceed with the chemo that is causing my neuropathy. So grateful! I don't need this to get any worse. I will go ahead with the other chemo today though, so at least I'm getting something. I had my CT last night, getting anxious for the results. Hope you all have a great day!

*Barb's Journal*
After I took Mikey to school, I headed back to Rachel's to wake her up for her shot. She was already up and eating

breakfast. After she was finished eating, we headed to the cancer center for chemo.

For most treatments she has her favorite nurse, Deana, who's one of the kindest, funniest, and most caring I've ever met. She makes the difficult experience of chemo somewhat bearable.

Rachel has been experiencing neuropathy in her feet caused by one of the chemo drugs. Because of her fall on Tuesday, the nurse practitioner made the call not give Rachel that drug today, which was a relief to both of us. She was worried about the numbness getting worse and maybe not going away.

Only receiving one chemo drug today made the appointment four hours instead of five or six.

I took her home and she took some pain meds and went to bed. I'm so grateful to God that this treatment is over and next week is an off week, so she'll get a ten-day break. I'm also praying she can gain some of her strength back.

Friday, October 4, 2019

*Barb's Journal*

Today is going to be a fun day for Mikey and me. His class is going to an orchard and I'm chaperoning. We're so excited!

I was able to ride on the bus with the students, which I so enjoyed. I sat with Mikey and his good friend Braylon. They wanted to sit next to the window, so I took the aisle seat. It was fun talking to Braylon. He said he's an only child and lives with his parents. He's a cute kid, and he and Mikey are the best of friends. I remember being in elementary school and having special friends.

The orchard was really nice. They had a huge barn that we all fit into for a lesson on growing apples. After the lesson we took a hayride around the property making one stop for apples and cider. When we got back to the front building, we went inside the store for donuts and more cider. After we ate we went outside to the play area. It wasn't long before the buses came to pick us up and take us back to school.

I'm thanking God for the opportunity to be a part of Mikey's school trip. It warmed my heart.

SATURDAY, OCTOBER 5, 2019

*Barb's Journal*

Before heading over to Rachel's I stopped at our favorite donut shop. When I was growing up, it was a Jack in the Box restaurant. My mom would take us sledding in the winter, and afterward we would go there for hot chocolate. Once it became a donut shop I would buy the kids birthday cakes there. A week before their birthday I would take them to order their cake. Then on the day of the party we would pick it up. I loved seeing the look on their faces when they saw the cake they had picked out. Every time I stop there for donuts it makes me smile with fond memories.

The weather was nice which allowed Mikey and me to spend most of the morning outside. He loves to ride his battery-powered F150 truck that Tim and I bought him for his birthday. I mainly bought it because for nine years I built F150 trucks at the Ford Rouge Plant. One day, when he gets bigger, I'm going to take him on the plant tour.

Rachel's friends came over for the afternoon, so Mikey and I headed to my house for the night.

I found some toys on the buy/sell/trade Facebook site and can't wait to give them to him. I bought a camper with all the accessories. I know how much he loves to camp so I'm sure he's going to love the toy.

We ordered pizza for dinner and settled in for an evening of watching movies.

Thanking God it was a good day for all of us.

SUNDAY, OCTOBER 6, 2019

*Barb's Journal*
We took Mikey to church this morning, and he was so happy to see his favorite teacher, Jared. Jared has a special heart for children, and he has been so patient and kind to Mikey. Mikey can be a handful, but it doesn't bother Jared one bit. He's one of the angels that God put into our lives during this difficult time.

So thankful to God for an amazing support system.

I dropped Mikey off at his house after church because Rachel was going to take him to a coed baby shower at her dear friend's house. When I opened her door and saw her lying on the couch, I knew she didn't feel well. She had been sick most of the night throwing up. This chemo is so hard to take. My heart breaks to see her so sick.

It was hard to leave her, but I needed to get groceries and do some laundry at my house, so I gave her a hug and a kiss on her cheek. I sure wish I could take all this sickness away, but the only thing I can do is make sure she is as comfortable as she can be and pray, pray, pray that God heals her.

MONDAY, OCTOBER 7, 2019

*Barb's Journal*
Got over to Rachel's at my usual 7:30 a.m. and Mikey was

already awake and ready to start the day. We did our usual routine: get dressed, brush our teeth, eat breakfast, and watch his favorite show, Tayo the Little Bus. We also sing songs. Rachel has the Alexa voice app. Mikey and I take turns playing songs and singing to them. It's a fun start to our day and always makes us smile and laugh.

After I took Mikey to school, I went back to Rachel's to wake her up for her 9:00 a.m. shot. She wasn't feeling good, so after her shot she went back to sleep until 11:00 a.m.

Once she woke up I gave her some meds for her stomach issues and she was able to eat some lunch. I feel so bad for her. She's sick almost every day. All I can do is try to encourage her to take meds for whatever is ailing her.

I pray, pray, and pray that God heals her.

Tuesday, October 8, 2019

*Barb's Journal*
Two friends from Rachel's work came to visit her this morning and it made her day. Sarah and Julie are true friends, and it's so good to see Rachel smile and laugh when they are over. They also bring yummy goodies, as well as gifts. Thanking God that He has given Rachel such an amazing group of friends who never forget her even though she's been off from work for six months now.

Wednesday, October 9, 2019

*Barb's Journal*
We had a busy morning. I went to Mikey's school at 9:30 a.m. for family hour to see what the kindergarteners are

learning. Mikey showed me all that he does every day. He showed me his tablet and all the programs he uses. We had yummy cider and donuts for snacks! Mikey's teacher said he's adjusted very well to school. She said he's happy and wants to be there. She also said he does everything she asks him to do. I'm one proud grandma!

Rachel went to dinner with some friends, which didn't go well. She felt light-headed and thought she was going to pass out. Thankfully the wheelchair was in the car so she could be wheeled out of the restaurant. Once she got home she went straight to bed. Anytime she makes plans to leave the house I get nervous. We never know how she's going to feel. Thanking God she didn't fall and was able to get home safely.

THURSDAY, OCTOBER 10, 2019

*Barb's Journal*

Rachel's very good friend and coworker Julie came over for breakfast. She's one of the sweetest women I know. Every time Rachel is in the hospital she makes sure she has everything she needs. Usually Rachel's on the same floor that Julie works on so she pops in all day long during her shift. I'm so grateful to God for the amazing support system that Rachel has. I believe her coworkers love her almost as much as I do!

FRIDAY, OCTOBER 11, 2019

*Barb's Journal*

After I got Mikey off to school and gave Rachel her morning shot, I headed to Bob Evans to meet a dear, dear friend.

# OCTOBER RALLY FOR RACHEL POSTS / BARB'S JOURNAL ENTRIES

Anna and I have been friends for many years. We unfortunately have in common the loss of our dear sons. Her son Andrew passed away in July 2, 2012. We say that we're in a club that no one wants to join. Anna is a very strong Christian, and whenever I talk to her, I leave feeling uplifted and inspired. I told her that she is one of the angels that God put in my life. Thank you, God, for my angel Anna.

SATURDAY, OCTOBER 12, 2019

*Barb's Journal*
After lunch I headed over to Rachel's to get Mikey and take him for a haircut and lunch. He's been getting haircuts every three weeks since he was less than a year old. His hair grows really fast and thick. Thankfully he's good when I take him, and afterward I reward him by taking him to McDonald's for lunch and playtime.

Rachel got us tickets to the Detroit Zoo Boo, but I wasn't sure if she was going to be able to go. She hasn't been feeling very good. After we got back from our errands, Rachel was all ready to go to the zoo. Woot, woot! We had an amazing time. Mikey loves the zoo and loves getting candy. We saw camels, peacocks, and reptiles. The entire zoo wasn't open, but what we did see was fun.

Mikey's older sister, Emily, and her boyfriend, as well as their son, Jayson, met us there. It was wonderful seeing them. Mikey loves Jayson. They had a good time being together.

Thanking God for giving Rachel a good day! God is so very good!

SUNDAY, OCTOBER 13, 2019

*Barb's Journal*
Tim and I went to church this morning and then met our dear friends Michelle and Mark for lunch. It was so nice to be able to spend some quality time with them!

I texted Rachel twice and she said she was doing good, which makes my heart smile. I don't like not seeing her today, but I know she needs to spend time with her husband and son. If something changes, she knows she can call me and I will be right over.

Thanking God Rachel is having a good day!

Monday, October 14, 2019

*Rally for Rachel by Rachel*
Hi all! I had a great weekend & stayed busy. My ankle is finally feeling better but both my feet are still numb. This week, Wednesday, I have an oncology appointment so I will get the results of my CT then we will discuss where we go from there with Tx. I will update as soon as I can. Have a great week!

*Barb's Journal*
After I got Mikey off to school, I headed back to Rachel's for her 9:00 a.m. shot. After her shot she said was tired and wanted to sleep, which she did until 11:00 a.m.

Once she got up I asked her what she felt like eating for lunch, and she said Culver's; their mint shake sounded good to her. Thankfully she was able to eat lunch and keep it down while we watched the DIY shows she loves so much.

I'm anxious for her oncology appointment on Wednesday. There's a lot riding on this appointment.

# OCTOBER RALLY FOR RACHEL POSTS / BARB'S JOURNAL ENTRIES

Tuesday, October 15, 2019

*Barb's Journal*

After I took Mikey to school, I went back to Rachel's to wake her up for her 9:00 a.m. shot. She said she was tired and went back to sleep.

I headed to the gym for an hour, and when I got back, she was up and dressed and ready to go to the cancer center for blood work. After her appointment she said she was hungry and wanted a coney dog at the hotdog stand in the next town over. It's a car hop so we didn't even have to get out of our car to eat. They have cold, frosty mugs that they serve root beer in. What an amazing treat. I love when Rachel is feeling well enough to eat out; we both enjoy our time together.

Wednesday, October 16, 2019

*Barb's Journal*

After I took Mikey to school, I headed to the cancer center in the next town over where Rachel's oncologist's office is. The doctor said the scans showed that the tumors in her pancreas, as well as her liver, had shrunk and that her cancer numbers were better.

In August they were 9,500 and had dropped to 4,700, which we were really pleased with. Rachel told him she didn't want to have the chemo drug that is causing her neuropathy in her feet, and he agreed that they could just use the one chemo drug for six weeks and then in eight weeks have another scan and see where we are. He reminded us that there is no cure. He also told her at any time if she wanted to stop the chemo and go on comfort care, he would do that for her. That was very hard to hear; both Rachel and I cried and hugged each other after the doctor left the room. My heart is aching for my precious Rachel.

Thursday, October 17, 2019

*Barb's Journal*
After I took Mikey to school, I headed back to Rachel's to wake her up for her shot. After her shot she said she was going to go back to sleep so I went to the gym for an hour.

When I got back to Rachel's, she was still in bed so I left her alone. At twelve thirty she got up to go to the bathroom and said she felt like staying in bed. I sat on her bed with her and we both cried. She's very depressed about her condition.

She said she wishes it wasn't her going through this, which I agreed. I said I wish it was me. I already have done everything I wanted to do in life, and she has her whole life ahead of her. I told her it was really unfair and I'm so sorry. She is undecided about what to do about the chemo. I told her that we have a good plan, which is only one chemo drug until December when she has another scan. I asked her if she could set aside her worry until December, and she said that she would try. I am truly powerless over this situation. All I can do is pray, which I do constantly.

Friday, October 18, 2019

*Barb's Journal*
After I dropped Mikey off at school, I went back to Rachel's, and to my surprise she was up and in the living room watching TV. She asked if I would take her to get her nails done, and

I said sure. I'm so grateful that she's trying to stay out of bed and have a better outlook on things.

After I picked up Mikey from school, we went to Rachel's to get his meds, clothes, and toys so he could stay the night with Tim and me.

The weather was really mild so we played outside for an hour and a half. Tim came home from work, and he and Mikey took turns riding Mikey's big wheel down the driveway. They had so much fun; it was so good to see Mikey having fun and being a little boy.

Thank you, God, that Rachel is doing better and it's rubbing off on Mikey. His emotional state has been wonderful. After his counseling appointment on Wednesday, he has turned a corner, and I am praising God for it. God is our healer!

Sunday, October 20, 2019

## *Rally for Rachel post from Rachel*

Hi all! I've been pretty emotional since my last doctors appt. We talked about how bad the neuropathy is and that we backed that chemo off, we talked about quality of life too, how important it is and it took me back to the what if's. What if I only do one chemo, will it help? What if I have to be put on the other chemo again to speed up the process of this stubborn tumor!? How will that effect my feet? Will I be wheelchair bound because I can't feel my feet/walk.

I want a good quality of life AND I want to get better. From here until December I will be getting chemo once a week, December 4th will be my next CT scan. Thankfully the side effects only last the first day then I am good. What is helping is me getting out & doing stuff with the family. Yesterday we went to my Dad & Karen's and went trick-or-treating in Howell and had a nice dinner at their house. Today we got out to lunch & sat outside for a few hrs. I am trying really, really hard to keep things as they were before I got sick, it is just hard because I am feeling weaker. I hate this cancer! Thanks for letting me vent.

Monday, October 21, 2019

*Barb's Journal*
After I dropped Mikey off at school, I went back to Rachel's to wake her up for her 9:00 a.m. shot. She said she was really tired so she went back to sleep until 11:00 a.m.

Once she woke up she said she is going to try to get out every day and asked if I would take her to get a cheesesteak hoagie. I said sure, and off we went. We had a really good talk. She said that she's decided to fight for Mikey. She said Mikey needs a mom, so she's going to make an extra effort to do things with him in the evenings. She brought tears to my eyes. Just last week she was so depressed, and I wasn't sure she would be able to pull herself out of the depression, but she has.

God is so very good! All the prayers that everyone has been praying are working. We serve a mighty God!

Tuesday, October 22, 2019

*Barb's Journal*
Rachel was very tired all day today. Yesterday she went out twice and did a lot of walking, which has wiped her out. All she wanted was to sleep, and for lunch she asked for a

grilled cheese sandwich. She's trying really hard to get out every day to build up her strength. She said when she fell a month ago and didn't have the strength to get up, she realized that she's going to have to make an effort to get some sort of exercise daily to build her strength back up.

WEDNESDAY, OCTOBER 23, 2019

*Barb's Journal*
After I got Mikey off to school, I went back to Rachel's to wake her up for her 9:00 a.m. shot, and to my surprise she was already up and ready for the day.

She needed to get blood work done, so she said, "Let's go get it out of the way." After her appointment I asked her if she felt like a treat, and she said yes; she wanted a strawberry refresher from Starbucks. I decided to get a hot apple cider with caramel and whipped cream. It was a nice treat for both of us.

For lunch she wanted Subway so that's where we went.

So grateful to God that I'm able to spend quality time with Rachel every day. It's such a gift.

THURSDAY, OCTOBER 24, 2019

Rally for Rachel post by Rachel as she checked into the cancer center

At my second home! Kicking cancer's butt one week at a time!

FRIDAY, OCTOBER 25, 2019

*Barb's Journal*
After I dropped Mikey off at school, I went to the 7-Eleven

to buy donuts for Rachel and me. I just love their cream-filled long johns, and Rachel likes anything chocolate.

When I got to her house, I was happily surprised to see her up and ready for the day. She said she slept really good and was feeling good. Thankfully the one chemo drug that she gets weekly doesn't have the horrible side effects she experienced with some of the other drugs.

Rachel's friend Marissa came to visit, and I overheard Rachel telling her that she knows that she's going to die from the cancer; she just doesn't know when. This hit me like a ton of bricks. Up until now she's been optimistic about getting well. I know that the survival rate is very low, but I'm still praying for a miracle.

Every morning on my way to Rachel's I drive by a church, and lately I have been pulling into the parking lot to pray. I know God is everywhere, but I have to believe that by praying in a church parking lot I'm getting closer to where He is. Also, I was listening to the actor Stephen Baldwin give his testimony on how he and his wife got saved. He said that in the morning and at night his wife prays while lying on the floor facedown. This morning I lay on the floor and prayed for Rachel's healing. After I got up from the floor, it felt like a weight had been lifted off my shoulders. I'm going to do this daily.

Thanking God today that Rachel is doing well. God is so good!

SATURDAY, OCTOBER 26, 2019

*Barb's Journal*

Rachel had a good day. She was able to get out and go to the movies. This was the first time since she was diagnosed that she was able to go out and have some fun. I'm so happy for her.

Tim, Mikey, and I went bowling and Mikey got a strike on his first roll. We couldn't believe it! Mikey was so excited!

SUNDAY, OCTOBER 27, 2019

*Rally for Rachel post by Rachel*
Hi all! This chemo is really treating me good! Minimal side effects, thank you Jesus! It's been a busy weekend but I am keeping up!

*Barb's Journal*
Went to church with Mikey and he had a wonderful time. After church I took him home and he went with Mark and Rachel to pick out pumpkins. He was so excited when I called to see how everyone was doing.

Rachel had a good day. She went to breakfast and then grocery shopping. She was able to use the electric shopping cart. She said it felt really good to get out of the house. This new regimen of chemo, which is less aggressive, is really agreeing with her.

MONDAY, OCTOBER 28, 2019

*Barb's Journal*
After I dropped Mikey off at school, I headed to Rachel's for her 9:00 a.m. shot, and to my surprise she was already up and had already taken her shot. She even fixed some breakfast. It makes my heart smile to see her doing so well.

I got Subway for lunch, and we watched our DIY shows, which we do whenever we are home in the afternoon. I nap most of the afternoon, which feels really good.

Thanking God today that Rachel is doing so well.

WEDNESDAY, OCTOBER 30, 2019

*Rally for Rachel post by Rachel*
Fun fact: when I'm at chemo my favorite treat is orange juice over ice (she posted a picture of her drink)

*Barb's Journal*
When I got to Rachel's, I saw that Mikey had thrown up and was not feeling well at all. Rachel contacted the school to say he wouldn't be there. I cleaned up Mikey and his bed and put him on the couch.

Rachel has chemo at 9:30 a.m., and I wasn't sure if Mikey would feel up to dropping Rachel off at the cancer center, but I took a chance and he tolerated it.

Rachel texted me at 11:30 a.m. to say she was done with her chemo.

Once she got in the car, she told me she talked to Caroline, the physician assistant, and she said that her cancer numbers had gone up 3,000, which is not good at all. They talked and Rachel decided she wants to get a second opinion, so Caroline said she would put a referral in for that. It was very emotional knowing that without the aggressive chemo that is so hard on Rachel, the cancer is going to continue to thrive. We both cried, and it left me feeling hopeless.

THURSDAY, OCTOBER 31, 2019

*Barb's Journal*
Today is Halloween and I volunteered to work with Mikey's class for their party.

I arrived at 9:30 a.m. and helped with an art project. I had such a good time. When it was Mikey's turn to do the project, he sat right next to me. He makes my heart full. At 10:30 a.m. the school had a parade of everyone showing off their costumes. There were some amazing costumes. All of the teachers were dressed up, which made the day even more special.

After the parade we went back to the classroom to finish the party. The teacher asked each student what their favorite part of the day was and Mikey said that the best part was having his grandma there, which made me cry. When I told Tim, he said it makes all the hard work I have been doing taking care of Mikey and Rachel worth it.

Thank you, God, that Mikey feels the love that I have for him.

Rachel had a full house for the evening. Her friends Tony and Melissa came over with Tony's famous spaghetti sauce that was amazing. They have a cute four-year-old, Caroline, whom Mikey loves playing with.

These two have trick-or-treated together for three years. It's a fun tradition. Rachel's paternal grandmother, Patty, and her husband, Leonard, came over, as well as Tim and my sister, Linda. We had a wonderful time. Even though it rained, we still went out for candy.

Thank you, God, for an amazing day!

CHAPTER 18

# November Rally for Rachel Posts / Barb's Journal Entries

FRIDAY, NOVEMBER 1, 2019

*Barb's Journal*
USUALLY WHEN I get to Rachel's in the morning, Mikey is awake, but not this morning. He was fast asleep. I felt bad having to wake him up. Yesterday was a big day so I thought he would be cranky, but he wasn't. He was excited to show me all his candy that he got last night.

Rachel got a call from the Karmanos Cancer Center in Detroit saying she has an appointment on November 12 at 9:00 a.m. We are praying that maybe there is more we can do to fight this awful cancer.

Rachel and I had a quiet day watching the DIY home improvement shows that she loves. I cherish the time I spend with her.

Thank you, God, and my amazing husband, Tim, who takes care of us financially so I can focus on my daughter and grandson.

NOVEMBER RALLY FOR RACHEL POSTS / BARB'S JOURNAL ENTRIES

S ATURDAY, N OVEMBER 2, 2019

*Barb's Journal*
Rachel had a good day. She was able to get out and take Mikey to Dave & Buster's to eat and play video games. She also was able to ride in the electric scooter at Sam's Club.
This makes my heart smile.

S UNDAY, N OVEMBER 3, 2019

*Barb's Journal*
Rachel hung out with Mikey and had a lazy day. Thank you, God, for the precious time she gets to spend with Mikey.

M ONDAY, N OVEMBER 4, 2019

Rally for Rachel post by Rachel
Hi all! Just a quick update. Since I have been off the one chemo that was causing neuropathy, my CA19-9 has sky rocked! So starting next week I will be put back on it. Also, next Tuesday we have an appointment with Karmanos, we are just exploring our options & curious to see what they have to say. This month is going to be crazy so please forgive me if I'm not updating. I will do my best to update when I can. Thank you all for the continued love & support. You guys keep me going!

*Barb's Journal*
After I took Mikey to school, I went back to Rachel's to get her up for her 9:00 a.m. shot. She said she was having a lot of pain in her liver area. She said it started last night so she took a Percocet and went back to sleep.

Rachel has decided to go back on the aggressive chemo. She called and talked to the nurse at the doctor's office. They said that would be fine, but it won't start until next week.

This concerns me because the aggressive chemo is so hard on her physically. Even though I'm concerned, it's her choice as to the type of treatment she gets because she's the one who has to go through it. It just hurts my heart to see her in pain and so sick. My heart is very heavy today.

TUESDAY, NOVEMBER 5, 2019

*Rally for Rachel post by Rachel*
Rachel shared a picture of a beautiful blanket Mark bought her

One of my sweet surprise I got in the mail today. Love you Mark & I love my new blanket #alwayscold

*Barb's Journal*
I fell into a deep depression after Rachel got the news that her cancer numbers were rising, and I was not able to journal again.

FRIDAY, NOVEMBER 8, 2019

*Rally for Rachel post by Rachel*
Hi to all my awesome supporters!! Happy Friday! If you have any holiday shopping to do for any friends, family, teachers or even to spoil yourself…check out this awesome fundraiser going on to help benefit our family. My friend Kelli is giving us 25% of her commission to help with food, bills, gifts for Mikey, etc! So many great products to choose from… you can check it all out here! Thanks so much!

# NOVEMBER RALLY FOR RACHEL POSTS / BARB'S JOURNAL ENTRIES

Sunday, November 10, 2019

*Rally for Rachel post by Rachel*
Hey all! I hope you all had a great weekend! Just wanted to give a quick update. I thought I had chemo last Thursday but it turns out I didn't, so that was a nice surprise, so I just got my picc care done while I was there. I got my blood drawn on Wednesday because I thought I had chemo this week. I looked at my CA19-9 and it was down by 3,000 points! I was pleasantly shocked! It had been going up so much I wanted to get back on the other chemo, well now I don't need to! Praise God! So we will continue to monitor and go from there. This week I have an appointment with Karmanos on Tuesday, sounds like it'll be a lengthy appointment but that's okay. Then on Thursday I have chemo in the morning. I hope you all have a great week & stay warm!

Tuesday, November 12, 2019

*Rally for Rachel post by Rachel*
Hi all! We just left Karmanos. We had a really good appointment and did not feel pressured. This stage 1 clinical trial is more of a last resort option, once we've exhausted all of our options this is something we may consider. It's very competitive, they only allow 3-4 people nationwide in at a time, so if a trial comes up you have to jump on it. I do qualify for immunotherapy which I was surprised but they looked at my results from my genetic counseling and they found out that, that may be an option. So as of right now we will continue with the chemo I'm already on because it's working.

## Wednesday, November 13, 2019

*Rally for Rachel post by Rachel*

Hey all! Just got done with my follow up appointment with the PA. I've been having sharp RUQ pain for about a week now. So she is worried it may be my gallbladder. She spoke with the Dr and wants a STAT CT to see of it's my gallbladder & make sure that the tumor is behaving itself. I also got bloodwork today. So my CT will be at 2, the Dr will call me later today once he gets the results. I will update when I hear something.

## Thursday, November 14, 2019

*Rally for Rachel post by Rachel*

Hey all! So I got the results back from my CT this morning. Gallbladder looks fine. But I still have some clots in my lungs, I don't have a cough or fever so they are not worried. If my gallbladder pain is not tolerable I need to go to the ER, but so far it is feeling better. I am getting chemo today, my CA10-9 is lower this week at 5524! Which is almost down 1000 points from last week & I didn't even have chemo last week! Praise God!

## Tuesday, November 19, 2019

*Rally for Rachel post by Rachel*

A go fund me account was set up to help Rachel's family
Rally for Rachel post by Mark
Rachel woke up with shortness of breath and pain in her side. Took her to St. Joe's ER. Will update when we know something. Prayers please.

## Update from Mark

Rachel is getting admitted to the hospital. She appears to have a new spot on her liver & possible pneumonia in her right lung. Love, prayers & support are needed.

Wednesday, November 20, 2019

## Rally for Rachel post by Rachel

Hey all! Today I was supposed to get fluid drained off my lung but when they used the ultrasound they saw that there was not enough fluid to take and not a safe place to poke. If they were to do it they could collapse my lung and then I'd need a chest tube. Not sure what plan B is yet but as soon as we find out I'll update.

Thursday, November 21, 2019

## Rally for Rachel post by Kate with a picture of her wearing a purple shirt

I'm wearing purple for Rachel! Who else? Post your pic below!

Many pictures of her coworkers at work wearing purple were posted on her page

## Update by Rachel

Hey all! So it looks like I have pneumonia in my lung again. So its IV antibiotics, Incentive spirometer, breathing tx. So grateful it's only pneumonia! I will be here in the hospital for another day or two. Thank you to all my visitors & sweet treats. You have all made my day a little brighter.

Friday, November 22, 2019

*Rally for Rachel post by Rachel*
   Going home this morning!

MONDAY, NOVEMBER 25, 2019

*Rally for Rachel post by Rachel*
   Hey all! Since I've been home from the hospital I've had a really poor appetite, tonight I was able to eat dinner! I was so happy! Also still fighting with pain in my lungs but keeping up with pain meds have helped. This week I have chemo on Wednesday morning. I'm looking forward to Thanksgiving especially pumpkin pie! Hoping I feel well enough to make it to the family events. Have a great week you all. I have so much to be thankful for this year.

WEDNESDAY, NOVEMBER 27, 2019

*Rally for Rachel post by Rachel*
   Good morning! I am at chemo and my numbers have gone up by 3000 points! So we added the other chemo back on. Please pray that it goes well & the neuropathy doesn't get worse. Have a great day!

THURSDAY, NOVEMBER 28, 2019

*Rally for Rachel post by Rachel*
   The devil wanted to keep me from Thanksgiving celebrations today. Yesterday, I was so sick and thought for sure I'd never make it out today. I took some pain medications, took a nap and by 8pm I felt like a new person.

This morning I woke up feeling great & I was able to make it to all 3 Thanksgiving celebrations! God is so good & he knew how special this Thanksgiving is for me and my family. I hope you all had a wonderful day with family.

CHAPTER 19

# December Rally for Rachel Posts

Wednesday, December 4, 2019

*Rally for Rachel post by Rachel*
 Can't come soon enough. (she posted an article about a cure for pancreatic cancer that is in the testing stage)
 Rally for Rachel post by Rachel
 Juice is gone now just waiting to be brought back for my CT
 Rally for Rachel post by Rachel
 Hey all! As you can see from my last post I had my CT today. Picc wouldn't flush so I had to have the IV team come & start one on me. As the contrast went in my arm, it got a really hard, large bump on it but the fluid was still going through & I felt warmth and all that. So now I've got to keep it elevated & ice/heat on and off for the next 12 hrs. Hoping it'll go down by tomorrow. This week is my off week for chemo! Tomorrow I go in for picc dressing change & Friday I have a follow up with my pcp. Have a great week!

Sunday, December 8, 2019

*Rally for Rachel post by Rachel*
Hey all! I hope you've all had a great weekend! I sure have!
This week I have a palliative care appt tomorrow, and on Wednesday I have an oncology appt to follow up on my CT, I'll be sure to update after that appt. I am sure I'll have chemo this week just not sure what day. I'm looking forward to this next weekend, we are making Christmas cookies! I love making them and we have plenty of help! Have a great week everyone!

Wednesday, December 11, 2019

*Rally for Rachel post by Rachel*
Praise report! Today I had my oncology appt & the CT showed that nothing has changed since the scan in October & are stable! Praise God! So we are going to continue on with the 2 chemo's & my next scan will be in 2 months.

Monday, December 16, 2019

*Rally for Rachel post by Rachel*
Hi all! I have had a few rough nights, not getting much sleep & just uncomfortable. Today mom helped me get all the Christmas presents wrapped! So that's a relief! This week I have chemo on Thursday @ 11:30. This weekend we will be celebrating Christmas with the mom's side of the family & then my dads side of the family. Praying I will feel well enough to enjoy it all. Have a great week!

Tuesday, December 17, 2019

*Rally for Rachel post by Rachel with a picture of her*
Well, my hair was growing like crazy for awhile, now it's all falling out again. I gotta say I'm kinda glad because I would have to start styling it pretty soon!

Thursday, December 19, 2019

*Rally for Rachel post by Rachel with a picture of the cancer center employees and tons of Christmas gifts for the family*
We are beyond blessed! The whole cancer center clinic adopted us for Christmas this year! I can't even describe how grateful I am to have such a great team take care of us! Merry Christmas!!!!

*Rally for Rachel post by Rachel*
Hey all! Today the WBC are .9! Too low to have chemo! So today I just got my picc care. Next chemo will be December 26th!

Monday, December 23, 2019

*Rally for Rachel post by Rachel*
Hi all! This week came quick! I knew Christmas would be here before I knew it. Tomorrow I go for bloodwork & thursday I have chemo. I hope you all have a wonderful Christmas with your family!

Thursday, December 26, 2019

*Rally for Rachel post by Rachel*

Hey all! Today I had chemo.

I had a hard time when I got home...full body ache & just felt like crap! So I took some medication and went to bed, I am feeling much better now.

*Rally for Rachel post*

So my tumor markers went up tremendously! Last week they were at 19,000 & today was over 33,000 so of course I'm freaking out! Dr did not put a note in so I called the office. They got back to me right away and said no notes were in but they were going to go ahead and page him so I could talk to him. I never received a call back, so I'm praying that no news is good news.

SATURDAY, DECEMBER 28, 2019

*Rally for Rachel post by Mark*

Asking for prayers for Rachel. She was up all last night vomiting. Today, she has been in bed unable to eat with some vomiting. Called oncology. They called in some meds. She was unable to keep it down. Now we are in the ER. Will update when we know more.

SUNDAY, DECEMBER 29, 2019

*Rally for Rachel post by Mark*

They gave Rachel 2 meds for nausea & hydrated her & sent her home. She is feeling a little better. Thanks for the continued prayers.

MONDAY, DECEMBER 30, 2019

*Rally for Rachel post by Mark*

UNBREAKABLE

Rachel had a rough night, last night. She was up most of the night vomiting. So...we're back in the ER. Will update when we know anything.

*Rally for Rachel post by Mark*
Update: Rachel is getting admitted to the hospital. They did a CT scan & either the tumor has grown or shifted & could be putting pressure on her stomach. They are going to scope her to get a better picture & see what to do next. Surgery is not out of the question. Right now we are asking for all the prayers we can get. Thank you

Tuesday, December 31, 2019

*Rally for Rachel post by Mark*
Update: The tumor has grown/shifted. It is putting pressure on Rachel's stomach. Looks like they are going to put a stint in & use radiation to shrink the tumor. Rachel's oncologist is taking her off chemo & putting her into an immunotherapy trial.

Please keep the prayers coming & have a safe & happy New Year.

CHAPTER **20**

# January Rally for Rachel Posts

FRIDAY, JANUARY 3, 2020

*Rally for Rachel post by Rachel*
Good morning all! So yesterday, I had my stint placed in my stomach to keep the opening open. When I woke up I was in a little pain, got pain meds and felt much better after that. I was also able to have a liquid diet & that went well. I don't feel like anything is getting lodged and everything stayed down. I had a pretty good nights sleep still here in the hospital. Today I got advanced to a soft diet, as long as that goes well it sounds like I can go home later this afternoon. Thank you all for all your prayers!

SUNDAY, JANUARY 5, 2020

*Rally for Rachel post by Rachel's*
Hey all! I came home from the hospital friday afternoon. Things have been going okay, I have soreness from time to

time with the stint being placed. The next 2 weeks are going to be pretty busy. I will start radiation tomorrow to shrink the tumor so it doesn't put so much pressure on my stomach, that is 5 days a week for the next 2 weeks then I will go on a trial for immunotherapy. The doctors have to present it to the tumor board this tuesday. I am not sure when I will start immunotherapy but I'll post an update when I know.

MONDAY, JANUARY 6, 2020

*Rally for Rachel post by Rachel*
Hi all! Just a quick update. I did not have my first radiation tx today. Today they only did markings & my first tx will be January 16th.

WEDNESDAY, JANUARY 8, 2020

*Rally for Rachel post by Mark*
Today didn't go as planned. Rachel had an oncology appointment today. We found out that she wasn't accepted into the immunotherapy trial we were hoping for. She still starts radiation next week. After that it is up in the air. Her doctor is going to contact the drug manufacturer about getting her the immunotherapy drugs on a compassionate basis. We have an appointment at Karmanos on Tuesday about getting on a trial there. Please keep Rachel in your prayers. We need all we can get.

SUNDAY, JANUARY 12, 2020

*Rally for Rachel post by Rachel*

Good morning all! I got a phone call Friday from the radiation nurse and I will start radiation tomorrow at 11:30. I am super excited to be starting earlier this week. I have been in a lot of pain this week. Praying the radiation will help and shrink that darn tumor! We also have an appointment with Karmanos on Tuesday.

Curious to see if they have any trials going on right now or within a month I can jump into. Have a great Sunday!

TUESDAY, JANUARY 14, 2020

*Rally for Rachel post by Mark*
Rachel woke up with shortness of breath. At hospital now. PRAYERS PLEASE!

*Rally for Rachel post by Kate*
It is with a heavy heart that I need to let everyone know that at 8:18am this morning Rachel earned her wings. Thankfully she did not suffer. Thank you everyone for all the love, support & prayers over the last 9 months. She is at peace with God now.

CHAPTER **21**

# Funeral

ONCE AGAIN I find myself at the funeral home making arrangements for my precious child's funeral. Once again I'm asking myself, why? Why my daughter? I've already lost two sons; couldn't I at the very least been able to keep my daughter?

All I can say is I'm completely devastated. I knew there was a big chance that she wouldn't survive, but I still held out hope that she (we) would get the miracle we were all praying so hard for. How am I going to go on without her? How's Mikey going to live without his mother? These are questions that I have no answers for.

Thankfully Tim had talked to Rachel before she passed and asked her what arrangements she would like if it came to that. Once we all got to the funeral home Tim relayed the information from Rachel to her friend Molly, who was handling the arrangements. Her parents own the funeral home and Rachel went to school with her, which made a very stressful situation a tiny bit better.

We decided to have the viewing on Friday from noon to 8:00 p.m. and the funeral on Saturday at 1:00 p.m.

## FUNERAL

I had previously contacted a dear family friend, Linda, who attends the church I grew up in and Rachel was baptized in to see if we could have the funeral there. Linda got with Pastor Alex, and he said that would be fine.

After we were done at the funeral home, we went to the church to talk to the pastor. He was amazing and made us all feel so welcome. The last time I had been in this church was for my dear mother Mary Lou's funeral several years prior.

I was raised in this church and have so many fond memories. It's a large church so I knew it could accommodate all the people who were going to attend.

After we were done, we all went back to Rachel's house to be with Mikey. The house was full of friends and family so as soon as I knew Mikey was okay, Tim and I went home.

We had to wait a few days until the funeral, so Tim and I went to Rachel's house every morning and spent the day with Mikey. Everyone was so wonderful bringing food and flowers. Many people sent gifts to Mikey, which was a good distraction.

On Friday we met at the funeral home at 10:30 a.m. so we could be there before everyone started to arrive. I knew that the next few days were going to be rough, and they were. Eight hours of talking to friends and family was exhausting. I'm not sure how many people attended, but the guest book had 260 signatures. Many were for families so I have no idea on the actual count.

So many of Rachel's coworkers came, and they all said what a special person she was and how she helped everyone that she came in contact with. My heart was full hearing all the wonderful stories.

Thankfully we had a lot of help with Mikey. Rachel's sister-in-law, Kate, never left Mikey's side. He would go downstairs to play with his toys; then he would run back upstairs to see his mom. She was such a trooper. I couldn't have visited with the people who came if I had to keep an eye on Mikey. One of Rachel's dear friends, Tasha, her amazing husband, and their daughter Izzy took Mikey to McDonald's for dinner, which helped out so very much. It was good that he could get away for a bit. Once he got back, bless Kate's heart, she was right back on the job of running after him.

It was good to see everyone and hear their stories, but by 7:00 p.m. I didn't know if I would be able to make it another hour. Thankfully God carried me through that hour. Tim and I said our goodbyes to everyone and headed home. I knew it was going to be a long night, but I was hoping I could get a few hours of sleep before we had to head to the church for the funeral.

It had started snowing during the night, and by the time we got up, we could see it had been quite a storm. And the snow was not letting up. We left early because we knew the roads were going to be bad. When we got to the church, they were plowing the parking lot, so we had to wait until they were finished before we could go in. I knew because of the amount of snow we were getting that many people would not be able to make it to the funeral.

Tim and I started to get phone calls and texts from people telling us how bad the roads were and that they tried coming, but it was just too bad. They all sent their love and said they were praying for us.

We had an hour of visitation before the funeral. So many dear friends came to support us. It was really heartwarming. When it was time for the funeral, Mark tried to get Mikey to go into the sanctuary, but he couldn't.

Thankfully, once again Kate came to the rescue and took him off to the playroom until it was over. This was a relief to me, as I didn't have to focus on Mikey; I could be present for the funeral.

We walked in and took our seats in front, and it was so very sad. The last time I had been in that church was for my mom's funeral, so, of course, memories of that came flashing back. Also, memories of Rachel being baptized came to me, which was comforting. Tim and I raised all three of our children in church, which also gives me comfort. I know that they knew God's voice when it came time for them to enter heaven.

We picked out some beautiful songs to be played, and then Rachel's precious grandpa Leonard did the eulogy. I wish someone had recorded it for us. He spoke so sweetly about Rachel and everyone who had touched her life. He truly brought tears to my eyes and the entire congregation.

Next my friend Mark read what I had written about Rachel:

"My precious Rachel, when you were born, you made my life complete. I had your brother Brent and then I got my baby girl. I am so glad that I dressed you in pink and frilly clothes when you were a baby because as soon as you were two or three you wouldn't let me put another dress on you. You were a strong-willed child, and I knew that when you grew up, I would never have to worry about you. You were a born leader at four years old. You took a dance class, and when we went to your recital, you were the leader of every dance. I was such a proud mom. You were fearless at three years old. You were the only kid in the neighborhood who could ride your bike without training wheels. You couldn't wait to be a mom, and when you had Mikey, you were a natural.

"I marveled at what a good mommy you were. When Mikey got sick last year, you were amazing. He came home from the hospital with ten different meds. I was amazed at how you laid them all out on the counter with your famous Post-it Notes in front of every bottle detailing the dose and how many times a day he needed to take them. I firmly believe that Mikey is still here with us today because of God's mercy and your amazing care. When you were diagnosed with cancer, you never let it get you down. You put a smile on your face and did whatever the doctors told you to do. You told me you were going to fight this with everything you had for Mikey.

> "You said last year Mikey fought for me, and now I'm going to fight for him. Many, many, many prayers went up for your healing, but God had a different plan. I'm not sure why He took you home, but I am so very grateful that I was able to be your mom for thirty-two years. You might be gone from this earth, but you have definitely made an impact for good on everyone knew you. I look forward to the day that I see you again, but until then you will forever be in my heart. I love you, baby girl, more than you will ever know.
>
> Mom"

The pastor gave an amazing sermon. He truly is an incredible man of God.

The funeral was over and they led us out into the hall where I lost it. I began sobbing loudly. I was so very devastated to be burying my precious daughter.

We all piled in our cars and headed to the cemetery to say our last goodbyes. It was still snowing, which Rachel would have loved because she loved the snow. The pastor said a few more words, and we all said the Lord's Prayer. Then we headed back to the church for a luncheon.

I don't even remember what we ate. All I know is that I needed to make sure Mikey was okay. I can't even tell you how long I stayed or if I ate. All I remember is when Mikey started to get restless, I headed out with him in tow.

Once I got Mikey home, I could breathe a sigh of relief it was finally over. Tim and I stayed with Mikey for a few hours; then we headed back to our house to get some rest.

CHAPTER **22**

# Life after Eight Weeks

EIGHT WEEKS AFTER Rachel passed away, her dear grandma Patty was diagnosed with stage 1 uterine cancer. She was scheduled for a hysterectomy on March 6th, so my sister, Linda, and I met them at the hospital the day of the surgery.

I arrived at the hospital first, and as I waited in the lobby, I talked to my dear friend Michelle on the phone. It was an emotional morning, as it was the first time I had been to the area of the hospital where Rachel had worked. My sister arrived so I said goodbye to Michelle. About fifteen minutes later, Patty and Leonard showed up and we headed to the surgery department. Patty was having trouble walking, but I didn't see a wheelchair that we could use, so we took several breaks for her to catch her breath as we all walked together. When we got to the surgery department, I had Patty sit down while I stood in line to check her in. When it was our turn, I had Patty come up to the desk. I was telling the clerk that Patty was Rachel's grandma, and I asked her if she knew Rachel. She said she did not, but she had heard a lot of wonderful things about Rachel. She told me that the day Rachel passed away the entire unit was distraught.

Patty's surgery went well, and we were so pleased that she got the VIP Rachel treatment! Everyone came in to see Patty and tell her how much they loved and missed Rachel; it was really beautiful. My precious daughter was so loved and missed.

The surgery went well, and they were able to remove the 1 mm tumor. Patty was able to go home the next morning, and a week later she got a call from her doctor saying that she did not need any further treatment. We are praising God for her miraculous recovery.

CHAPTER **23**

# Life after Nine Months

IT'S BEEN NINE months since my precious Rachel gained her wings and went to be with the Lord. Some days it feels like nine months, and other days it feels like there is no way it has been that long. It seems just like yesterday that she was still here with us.

In March, life as we knew it changed yet again with the COVID-19 virus that left us with a global pandemic. Mikey's school closed and I became his teacher. Let me first say that teachers are amazing and they do an awesome job with our youth. They deserve gold medals for all they do on a daily basis to help our young people thrive. Mikey has been blessed with the most amazing teachers in his short education history. I know that God has had his hand on him since before he was born. I can see the special care that He has taken to make sure Mikey has the most amazing support system.

Virtual learning has been very hard on Mikey. He's a very busy six-year-old who does not like sitting in front of a tablet. Thankfully his teacher and his teacher supports have streamlined his daily tasks. On Thursday, October 22, he will go back to in-person learning. He will attend class on

Monday, Tuesday, Thursday, and Friday in the afternoons with Wednesday being a virtual day at home. We are both looking forward to him going back—me more than him!

It's now fall, which was one of Rachel's favorite seasons. Everywhere I look I am reminded of her, which is a blessing most of the time but sometimes grieves my soul.

She should be here with us going to the orchard and picking out pumpkins. Mikey is having a lot of memories of her. His most vivid fall memory is when he, his dad, and his mom went to a local pumpkin stand last year. Rachel was too sick to get out of the truck so Mark and Mikey picked out pumpkins as she looked on from the truck. She was such an amazing mommy; even when she was at her worst, she made an effort to be with her precious Mikey and Mark. I am so very thankful that Mikey has such wonderful memories of their precious time together.

Most days I am functioning well, but on Sunday when Mikey is with his dad, the pain of losing Rachel can be almost too much to take. If you have lost a child, you understand. If you have not, you will never know the pain, and I don't want anyone to have to join this sad, sad club that so many of us are forced to be in. Grief is a tricky thing to maneuver. My day can be running smoothly and, all of the sudden, bang! It hits me that she's not here and she's never coming back. Our new reality without her is so very sad. Every day when I get up, I ask God for help. Help keeping the anxiety down, help taking care of my busy Mikey, and help to not become a bitter person. I figure if I have to be on this earth without my precious Rachel, I'm going to make sure her death is not in vain. I'm going to tell everyone who will listen that the only reason I've been able to function is because of my faith in God. He carries me when I cannot walk.

I love the poem "Footprints in the Sand." It sums up my life right now.

**Footprints in the Sand**

One night a man had a dream. He dreamed
he was walking along the beach with the Lord.

Across the sky flashed scenes from his life.
For each scene he noticed two sets of
footprints in the sand: one belonging
to him, and the other to the Lord.

When the last scene of his life flashed before him,
he looked back at the footprints in the sand.

He noticed that many times along the path of
his life there was only one set of footprints.
He also noticed that it happened at the very
lowest and saddest times in his life.

This really bothered him and he
questioned the Lord about it.

"Lord, you said that once I decided to follow
you, you'd walk with me all the way.
But I have noticed that during the most
troublesome times in my life,
there is only one set of footprints.
I don't understand why when
I needed you most you would leave me."

The Lord replied:

"My son, my precious child,
I love you and I would never leave you.
During your times of trial and suffering
when you see only one set of footprints,
it was then that I carried you."

—Carolyn Joyce Carty

CHAPTER **24**

# A Special Note to Parents Who Have Lost a Child

I HAVE ENDURED many losses and difficult times in my life, but I have to say that losing a child has been the worst loss I have ever experienced.

It was such a shock to my system that I didn't know where to turn. I knew in my head that they were gone, but my heart couldn't process it. The first year was a haze; I just went through the motions and cried every day. The second year was extremely painful because my heart caught up with my mind, and I knew they were never coming back.

What I tell a grieving parent is to be gentle with yourself. This is not something that is going to get better right away. It took me years to process my losses and still I can cry at the drop of a hat. My husband says you never get over the loss but you learn to live with it. I completely agree with this statement.

One of the greatest gifts that came to me is my therapist, Mary Sue. I started seeing her after I lost my youngest son, TJ. She also lost a child so she truly gets me. I have told her many

# A SPECIAL NOTE TO PARENTS WHO HAVE LOST A CHILD

times, and this is the truth, she saved my life. I do not believe I would be doing as well as I am without her.

There are many grief groups available to join, and I encourage you to reach out and find one that works for you. I'm so very grateful to Josh and Amber who started the group Proud Parents of Loss after the loss of their beautiful baby girl, Harper.

PPL has been instrumental in my healing, and I will forever have a special place in my heart for this brave couple who reach out to others in such an amazing way. It is hard to talk about my losses, but I find it very helpful to talk with people who have also lost a child. They understand in a way that no one else can.

CHAPTER **25**

# Family and Friend Memories

*Mark, husband*

One of my favorite memories of Rachel from a Facebook post of hers.

Rachel speaking, "This is too good not to share...went to autorama today...for 10 hrs! By the end my feet hurt, I'm hungry, my lips are chapped, and I'm exhausted! Thankfully my parents took Mikey overnight. Mark and I go to dinner at Outback, and as we are leaving I realize we never touched the bread! So I go to put it in my purse and Mark is about to have a heart attack, asking me what I am doing and why am I putting it in my purse. I say, 'Wait! I have a bag,' and I pull out a plastic grocery bag and put it in there! Mark just left me!"

*Mikey, son*

My favorite memory was going to Disney for my fifth birthday and riding the Slinky Dog Ride with my mom and dad.

*Barb, mom*

My favorite memory is being with her when she gave birth

to Mikey. As long as I can remember she wanted to get married and have a baby, so on February 7, 2014, her dream came true. She was an amazing mommy.

## Tim, dad

My favorite memories are jet boating and NASCAR races. My fondest one was taking her to the Daytona 500.

Barb bought us tickets for Christmas, and she was so excited to be going. Her favorite driver was Jeff Gordon, and he won the Daytona 500 that year. She could not have been happier.

## Mary Jane, mother-in-law

I was thinking about Rachel and how much I enjoyed my time with her. She always made me laugh.

Rachel and Mark loved Black Friday shopping. I was never a fan of shopping on that day. I had never gone into any store on Black Friday and vowed I never would. Well, that changed when I was cornered by Rachel. Rachel and Mark had planned what stores they were going to shop, and there was one place they needed to go, but it was not on their schedule. This is where Rachel approaches me with the idea. Why don't I go to Pump It Up to get their Black Friday deal for Mikey's birthday party? One guilt trip laid on me for that sweet boy's birthday. So there I was on a cold, windy day standing in line. We got it! Number five. Rachel knew how to get her way. I kidded her about how she got this old lady who had never entered a store on Black Friday to stand in line outside before the store even opened. Love her!

## Gary, brother-in-law

I felt like my daughter, Hannah, and Rachel had a special connection that you could see when they were together. They were both full of sass and eye rolls. I know Rachel always loved picking out clothes for Hannah, and she loved getting the clothes from Aunt Rachel.

### Kate, sister-in-law

I loved how thoughtful she was! I remember she was joking one year at Christmas that Graham was getting socks and underwear, and the next year she wrapped up some socks and underwear and pretended that was his present.

### Leonard and Patty, grandpa and grandma

Rachel made us feel so special; she reserved Sundays for us. We would visit and have dinner together. During the Christmas season, we would make Buckeye Candy with her and Mark. We would roll out many peanut butter balls and dip them in chocolate. Rachel would make enough to sell. During the early days of dating Mark, she said she was going to make him dinner. She asked her grandma to make her famous meat loaf, which she passed off as her own. The dinner was a hit! Several weeks later Mark asked her to make him some meat loaf, so she had to confess and tell him she didn't make it, her grandma did!

### Betty, aunt

Bill's Hot Dog Stand in Ypsilanti has been around forever. Ken and I took our two sons to it often. Who doesn't like hotdogs and root beer served in their vehicle? One of my favorite memories of Rachel is seeing pictures of her, her husband Mark, and son Mikey also going to Bill's. Every generation realizes that this is a special family place.

I first met Rachel when she was ten years old when Tim, my nephew, invited me over for dinner. It was so wonderful to see Tim and Barb, Rachel's mother, get together. Barb had two

# FAMILY AND FRIEND MEMORIES

children, Brent and Rachel, and Tim had one son, TJ, and they combined their lives and it worked. Even then Rachel wanted to be a nurse, and she became one.

She loved her family and I remember how they always celebrated birthdays and holidays 100 percent.

Rachel met Mark and they decided to be married in a chapel in Las Vegas. My husband, Ken; my sister, Lil; and I were there for their October wedding.

Rachel lost her brother Brent and later TJ. So sad, and yet she and Mark had Mikey. Mikey was loved and fit right in.

The visits of Mikey, Rachel, and Mark to the hotdog stand are immortalized on Facebook. So too are so many other happy pictures of birthdays, trips with grandparents Tim and Barb, New Year's gatherings, Thanksgiving...too many to recall. Mikey loved it all.

Then Mikey got a rare childhood disease. He almost died. His family surrounded him and he survived, and he thrives today.

Rachel developed stage 4 pancreatic cancer. She continued to live fully each day. Barb and Tim were there for her. Mark posted updates on her progress, and we all prayed. But God took this angel to heaven. She lives on through Mikey and Mark. Barb and Tim are very close to them.

There is no explanation as to why this cancer is so deadly. All I know is that this sadness is lasting, but we still have our memories of Rachel. All we can do is continue to do as Rachel did and live one day at a time. Each day is all the time we have. And we can still take time to laugh. Mikey is growing up strong and happy. Through his family he will always know his mom as they share their stories about her.

I am honored to be part of this project. Betty Cotner

*Linda, aunt*

My favorite memory is how thoughtful she was when she was working at the hospital and a friend or family member was there. She would always check on them on her break and let me know how they were doing.

*Nancy, aunt*

I remember how excited she was to hold her cousin Drew when she was born. She was just staring at her and saying how tiny she was.

I knew from the minute that she was pregnant with Mikey what an amazing mother she was going to be.

*Rhonda, aunt*

My favorite thing about Rachel was her smile; her beautiful smile lit up the room. Rachel's smile and personality had a way of making even the darkest days seem brighter. And she was a force to be reckoned with if you hurt someone she loved. I sure do miss her beautiful soul.

*Suzy, aunt*

Her binky purse loaded with pacifiers and those sweet curls is a memory that always comes to mind. Her talking with the pacifier between her teeth makes me smile.

I think the memory that makes my heart beat fast is the first year after Mike and I divorced and she told me I will always be her aunt. I was so very touched and still think of that and the love she gave.

*Trudy, aunt*

I have many fond memories of her. One of the earliest was sitting in Big Boy with Mom; she had to be about six to nine months old.

I gave her a package of crackers that came with Mom's soup. Apparently I didn't have a toy for her to play with, so I gave her the bag because I knew the noise would entertain her for a time. But I got engrossed with talking to Mom and didn't notice that she was very quiet. I looked down and saw that somehow she had gotten the bag open and she was licking the salt off the crackers, looking adorable with her eyes wide open and her little tongue licking away. Mom and I couldn't stop laughing.

Another memory that comes to mind was when she was about three or four years old. She liked to play hide-and-seek, so this time Grandpa Ray said he'd play. She went running in the house looking for a place to hide while Grandpa started to count. When he hit ten, he said, "Okay, ready or not, here I come." I was following behind him, and when we reached the bottom of the stairs, he yelled, "Rachel, where are you?" By this time we were in the kitchen. She yells back, "I over here." Before we really saw her, we knew where she was because we could see her feet sticking out from the curtains. Dad and I had a really good laugh.

*Randy, uncle*

My fond memory of Rachel is when she just began working at the hospital and was still single. She asked to come see me. I told her I would drive to see her, but she wouldn't hear of it. She wanted to come out to see me. Even meeting me halfway wasn't an option. Nancy and I had brunch with Rachel. Her heart was so big, giving, smiling. So much time had passed, but we picked up as if we saw her the day before. We laughed about some fun times, her as a small child, growing up etc. We laughed about so many things. She made our time visiting about her and me, not any troubles she was having. I still remember her hug goodbye.

So you know, I have not deleted the IM messages Rachel and I had a couple of weeks before she passed. Refusing to do it allows me to read the messages often. I smile when I read them, but it makes me sad as well. But our lunch together was typical Rachel, always giving and making it easy for the other person!

*Alex, cousin*

My memories are the crazy fun rides to school. We would crank the radio. She would scare me with her driving. We would stop for food and barely make it to school on time. LOL

*Anthony, cousin*

My favorite memory is when Rachel, TJ, and I would go to the Rolling Hills Water Park.

*Elizabeth, cousin*

I enjoyed all the times she would pick me up and we would go shopping.

*Terri, cousin*

I can say that Rachel was always so caring and supportive of everyone she knew. She supported my business venture in 31 Gifts and Handbags, hosting several parties with me. She introduced me to her friends and coworkers too. Rachel always welcomed everyone into her home with open arms!

She was so generous to others, especially with her time and attention.

She truly cared about everyone she knew, and she made you feel it! She always had a pleasant demeanor, was always smiling and easy to talk to, and loved to laugh. She really did light up a room! I don't think she had a mean bone in her body; I certainly appreciated that about her!

FAMILY AND FRIEND MEMORIES

## *Alicia, friend*

My memory is her bravery and kind heart, and she always made really good peanut butter balls at Christmas.

## *Amanda T., friend*

My favorite memories are when we went to sixth grade camp together. We shared a room. We wanted to share a bunk bed, but my cousin was in the same room as us, and my cousin had a meltdown because she was scared. Rachel was nice enough to give up her bed so my cousin Meghan could be near me (she didn't like to be away from home, so her mom made sure we were in the same room). I remember we were able to pick someone that we wanted to buddy up with in the room, and Rachel and I ran to each other and said that we wanted to be roommates.

Going to church with you guys is another memory I loved about Rachel. My family has never been church-going people, but I enjoyed going with you guys.

I remember staying the night and having the biggest crush on Brent, LOL. Side note: He was so, so, so gorgeous.

Arguing (but not really arguing) about NASCAR: I would always tell her, this is not a sport, this is so boring, watching a guy drive around in circles. It was always so fun messing around with her because she loved NASCAR so much, all thanks to Tim. She always talked about how Tim and she bonded over NASCAR. She would tell me, if I could get you to go to one NASCAR race with me, you would love it and it's more exciting in person than on TV. I always did hope to go with her one day so I could understand her excitement since I am a huge sports person.

I remember when she got her own trailer in Rawsonville Woods, I came over to hang out and stay the night, and she had this big cutout of a NASCAR driver (if I remember correctly he was her and Tim's favorite guy).

Rachel and I definitely fought like sisters, but we loved each other so much.

### Amanda B., friend

The first time I met Rachel was about a week after my son was born, and she came over with Mark to meet him. I was a little anxious meeting her since I had just given birth and wasn't feeling like myself yet. Rachel put my mind at ease from the moment I met her with her beautiful smile and a big hug. She was so sweet and kind to me, even bringing a gift for my son. We clicked right away, and when she left, I told my husband that Mark found a good one. Rachel would check on me and let me know she had baby fever and would come over to visit and hold Cameron. This was the start of a wonderful friendship. Even though Rachel is gone, this and many other memories I will always hold close to my heart.

### Tom, friend

Rachel was such a nice person. I always enjoyed going to the Woodward Dream Cruise with Rachel and Mark. She was so happy to

be there, and I always enjoyed talking with her. Even though it's not the same without her being there, I know she is still with us in spirit.

### Anna, friend

I only met Rachel twice, but I know her mother, Barb, very well. The first time I met Rachel was to take a meal over for her and her family.

I had reached out to Barb to see how I could help. I will be forever grateful that Rachel allowed me the gift of bringing a meal to her. When I arrived, I could see how tired she was, and yet she was so gracious. Rachel was sitting in the living room, and as Barb was putting the food I brought into the kitchen, I was able to spend some time talking with her. Even though Rachel was so sick with cancer and cancer treatments, she asked how I was doing. I felt comfortable enough with her to share that I was struggling with something very painful in my life. I still remember the peace I felt in her living room as the three of us prayed together.

The second time I saw Rachel was when Barb and I went to breakfast. We had planned to go together, just the two of us, but Rachel had asked to join us. I had enjoyed her company so much the first time I met her that I was very happy that she was coming. Once again Rachel asked how I was doing, and I responded honestly, telling her things were the same. I could see by her expression that she truly cared and was saddened by my situation, and once again she offered to pray for me. I marveled at her generous spirit and her ability to care about what was going on in my life when she was suffering so greatly.

She wasn't able to finish her breakfast, and she was clearly exhausted, yet she remained joyful. Later I was reminded of a movie I had watched where the main character's father was in the hospital dying. The father had been a very difficult man but had experienced a change of heart at this point in the movie. Another man talked briefly and prayed with the father. Afterward, in the hallway, the son asked him what he had talked about with his father. The man replied that when a person is gravely ill is when they are closest to God, and he knew God would hear his prayers. I believe God heard Rachel's prayers, and I am forever grateful for the opportunity to have known her, if only briefly.

### *Ashley, friend*

I have so many great memories of Rachel that it is almost impossible to just pick one. I will always remember our summers together. That was such an amazing feeling when school would let out for the summer. We would plan sleepovers and sing our hearts out to NSYNC. We worked at Wiard's Orchard together and rode our bikes down the dirt roads to get there. All the times I was able to go up north with you all was such fun; I will never forget it. I will never forget Rachel and her wholehearted smile and laugh.

### *Brittney, friend*

One night we were coming back from Cabela's and there was construction. She was driving a bit too fast and a cop was sitting at the side of the road and flashed his lights. I'm sure both our faces were priceless to see, but thankfully he didn't come after us. We spent many days out at Waterloo with friends, sitting and singing around the campfire.

We spent many hours driving around just because we could and always seemed to end up at Applebee's splitting a dessert.

### *Carol, friend*

A note to Rachel's son, Mikey:

Mikey,

I met your mom and dad when you were just a baby. They would bring you to my office in your car seat. They were just so excited to have their little boy. We went looking for the perfect home; their requirements were a good family neighborhood with a park for you to play in, close to family and grandparents so they could visit and be an important part of your life.

Once we found your home, they were so excited about getting your room ready for you. They picked special paint to make sure the colors would be perfect so you would have a special place to enjoy for years to come.

Mikey, in your mom's own words, you are your mom and dad's "true superhero"! They were so excited to let everyone know Mikey is in remission!

The family was so excited to have a family vacation at Disney World.

When I look at the pictures, you have the most beautiful smile that you inherited from your mom and dad. Every single picture shows you with your big smile and your mom with her beautiful smile. Every time I saw your mom, she had that beautiful smile.

She would want you to keep that smile and enjoy life to the fullest and have the best life you can have. Your parents are what we call "good people" who deserve the best! What a special family you have, always looking at the best part of life.

Your mom will always be with you in your heart because she is such a special person and loved you so much.

Remember what a special person you are! Your mom, dad, and you have a special place in my heart.

Carol

## Donna, friend

I never met Rachel, but I followed the journey as Mikey was sick. Then I tried to send encouraging words, but it's so hard to know the words except to pray. My dear aunt Ruth highly believed in prayer cloths and always kept one with her. When she passed away a few years ago, my cousin gave me a few blouses of hers and we cut them into squares to share with family and friends and anyone needing prayer. I sent one to Rachel, and we kept checking for it to arrive, but it never did. I thought, devil, you can try to stop prayer and kind gestures, but I won't stop. I messaged Rachel and said I'd send another one. This time she got it and thanked me and said she was going to keep it in her purse. I admired her strength and faith. I just wish the outcome could have been complete healing.

*Julie, friend*

I had the pleasure of hosting a coworker baby shower for Rachel at my house. She was so excited to become a mom. She was so appreciative for all the love, support, and gifts she got from everyone. Having Mike was her greatest accomplishment. She loved being a mom; she wanted nothing more than to give him the best life possible.

*Melissa, friend*

Rachel was folding Michael's infant socks after work one evening and looked dog tired. I asked her how she found the energy to do it all, and she smiled at me and said once this is done, we can hang out. I said what about Michael? How is he going to fall asleep? She turned off the lights and said, "Go to sleep now." I kid you not; he put his head down and fell asleep. I was amazed. Every time I came to visit, she was always working with Michael's speech or doing puzzles. He was her number one priority, and she showed me what it meant to be a good mother in a more relatable way than internal knowledge. Her patience and good humor are the reward I was left with. When I think of Rachel, I tend to remember her as a mother. This was where she excelled. That and the vanilla-chocolate popcorn she made.

## FAMILY AND FRIEND MEMORIES

### *Myszka, friend*

So all of us in the PCUA knew Rachel hated dentures. We got these raspberry-filled teeth and put them on her birthday cake to surprise her. She laughed and said we were not very nice. Those teeth are still in our freezer with her name on them.

### *Sara/Todd, friends*

Sara overheard Rachel talking at work about moving, and Sara asked if she needed help. Rachel said sure, and Sara proceeded to tell her that she and her husband, Todd, would be glad to help. Rachel said you haven't even asked Todd if he's available, but Sara said she was recruiting him anyway. It ended up being a running joke that Sara volunteered her husband for events without ever asking him beforehand.

Todd is a car guy and so are Rachel and Mark, so they decided to all go to the racetrack in Norwalk, Ohio. Rachel was so excited about their one-dollar ice cream. She told Sara, "You might have to stand in line for a while, but the ice cream is delicious and only a dollar." They had a wonderful time eating ice cream and watching the races.

### *Stephanie, friend/bowling league partner*

Rachel and I always talked about going up to the line to throw our bowling ball and laughed about if we tripped over the line because the bowling alley lanes were slick, and how we thought it would be funny to slide down the lanes like the bowling balls. We talked about how we would go down the lanes sideways so we could strike all the pins out with our bodies. LOL, the mind of kids.

### *Jamina, friend*

In seeing the beautiful mother/daughter relationship that Rachel and I had, Jamina penned a poem about her mother titled "Momma."

Virgin beauty, no need for makeup
Right hand holding early life on her hip.
Nurturing, later, with tender devotion
Breast feeling in the dark, flying sky.

True love ahead, beyond the everlasting sun,
A brown-skinned GI waiting in Detroit.
Both enigmas to each other's desires,
Their television deciphering broken English.

Three more soon to come from her womb's aching,
Lifting and rocking, darning and crocheting,
Mornings with hot coffee pulled to her lips.
On special occasions, Maybelline lashes and lipstick,

My mother's hands, stirring, pushing, and steering
Oatmeal and strollers and our '55 Buick.
Daily errands run with dangling cigarette,
Always empty white bread while budgeting pennies.

Photographs of well-scrubbed children and his boats,
Plastic and linen covers meant to save furniture.
Red knuckles and scrub boards, hanging laundry.
Cleanliness next to Godliness, she tells us with a sigh.

### *KC, friend*

Rachel was so kind to me when I first started to work at the hospital. She went out of her way to make sure I was doing okay and made me feel like we had been friends forever. She was such a genuine, fun person, and I always looked forward to working together. We would be running the pre-op and PACU with smiles and rolling our eyes to make it through some shifts.

When she met Mark, she was so giddy when she talked about him. You could tell she knew she had met the one. She was just glowing and all smiles when she talked about him.

When she first found out she was pregnant with Mikey, we were working the same shift, and she snagged a pregnancy test from the supply closet and took the test right there at work. When she came out, she was ecstatic. She had tears in her eyes and couldn't wait to share the news.

## *Kathleen M., friend*

Rachel was such a sweet friend to K. C. She came to our house for a makeup party and brought Mikey. She was just smitten with Mikey, and you could tell he adored his mom.

Another memory was when my father-in-law had open heart surgery and she was working in the waiting room that day. She had set up ahead of time to make sure he had the best nurses, and she met us with homemade chocolate chip cookies. She was just the sweetest to my family.

## *Lindsay, friend*

I remember the songs we sang when we were little like "Consider the Lilies" and "As Small as I Am." The one I remember for sure doing with Rachel was "Thank You," which we sang and used to sign to the words as well. My mom has a picture of the three of us (me, Rachel, and Lindsay) doing it, wearing the mime makeup and everything.

### Sarah, friend

Rachel was always a delight to have come stay with us. I remember her and Ashley laughing often.

There are so many memories of the girls together growing up. One that sticks out is when we had the blackout in 2003. Rachel, or we called her "Rachie," stayed the weekend with us. We had a saying that we survived that blackout of '03 with Rachie. When she got her new Mustang, she came over to give us a ride in it. Taking the girls shopping in the mall, getting our nails done. I sure miss her and her contagious laugh. Forever in our hearts.

### Tasha, friend

Rachel was the glue that held PACU together. She's still the standard that we measure all of our PACU clerks against. No one can fill her shoes. We were just talking about her yesterday. We have this new clerk who doesn't know how to highlight our fallout, and we said this wouldn't be Rachel approved. LOL.

We still don't have Post-it Notes out and available for people, LOL.

(Rachel was the queen of Post-it Notes.)

So many movies, dinners, spending New Year's Eve with her!

We surprised her for her birthday with candy dentures on her cake. We all loved to harass her so much when there were patients with dentures, so it only made sense to do this for her birthday! We had everyone in on it. They are still in our work freezer; no one is allowed to touch them or throw them away!

### Tracie, friend

I will never forget our Christmas plays at church and

memories in general of running around playing at church. Those were the days, the best!

## *Wendy, friend*

I have many wonderful memories of Rachel. There were so many jokes, laughs, and fun times in pre-op and post-op waiting room shenanigans. Visiting her when she was in the hospital and making sure she was getting good care, joking about our families, kids, and husbands. Just so many good memories.

CPSIA information can be obtained
at www.ICGtesting.com
Printed in the USA
JSHW021942100822
29116JS00005B/24